Anatomy
of the
Ship

The Destroyer
THE SULLIVANS

Anatomy
of the
Ship

The Destroyer
THE SULLIVANS

Al Ross

Naval
Institute
Press

Frontispiece
1. This August 1945 photo depicts *The Sullivans* in Measure 22 and provides a clear view of the additional ECM antennae fitted to the aft 40mm platform. The radar dish for the Mk 63 unit is just visible on the waist quad 40mm.

USN via A D Baker III

© Al Ross 1988

First published in 1988 by
Conway Maritime Press Ltd
24 Bride Lane, Fleet Street,
London EC4Y 8DR

Published and distributed in the United States of America and Canada by the Naval Institute Press, Annapolis, Maryland 21402.

Printed and bound in Great Britain

Library of Congress Catalog Card No. 87-63031

ISBN 0-87021-617-1

Contents

AUTHOR'S PREFACE

The purpose of this book, indeed the entire *Anatomy of the Ship* series, is to provide the modeler and ship enthusiast with extensive graphic and descriptive material on a particular ship or ship type. As a result, text dealing with the developmental or operational aspects of the ship are limited. This is not to diminish the importance of these subjects; rather, it is simply not the focus of the book. For those interested in the operational and developmental aspects of the *Fletcher* class destroyers, there are a number of excellent texts available, including:

Friedman, Norman. *US Destroyers: An Illustrated Design History.*
Harmon, J Scott. *USS Cassin Young (DD 793).*
Raven, Alan. *Fletcher Class Destroyers.*
Riley, John. *United States Navy Destroyers of WWII.*
Walkowiak, Tom. *Warship Data 1: USS Kidd (DD 661).*

Further information, and rather fascinating reading, dealing with the development of the *Fletcher* class DD may be found in the General Board Studies of 1940 and 1942, available on microfilm from the Naval Historical Center in Washington, DC.

Most of the descriptive text and drawing references were drawn from a variety of official manuals and plans prepared by BUSHIPS, BUORD, and Bureau of Construction and Repair, as well as photographic references.

ACKNOWLEDGEMENTS

Books of this nature require extensive research, a task made much easier and far more enjoyable through the efforts of a large number of people who graciously provided assistance. To these individuals, the author wishes to extend his heartfelt gratitude and appreciation. Among the many individuals helping out, and in no particular order, were: A D Baker III, who provided many excellent photos and BUSHIPS drawings; Dr Norman Friedman; Charles Crabbin, who provided the difficult-to-obtain references on the engineering plant; Tom Walkowiak, who loaned me that great manual on the 3in/50; Dr Dick Hughes; Robert Cressman, who provided the service history of *The Sullivans*; Karl Kalb and Pat Ross, both of whom spent time photographing *The Sullivans* and the *Kidd*; Alan Raven; Dr Dean Allard and his staff at the Naval Historical Center; Jim Swinnich, curator of the Buffalo Naval Park where *The Sullivans* is on display; John Lambert, who got me into this mess in the first place; and Diane, Jessica and Jim, my family, who tolerate the time it takes to do this sort of thing.

Introduction

The *Fletcher* class destroyer was the result of the 1940 General Board studies which sought a replacement for the *Sims* and *Benson* class destroyers of the late 1930s, which had displayed a number of deficiencies in the areas of stability and speed. A new design was needed to keep pace with the new carriers and battleships then on the drawing boards. After rejecting an initial series of proposals based on the earlier designs, the General Board received from the Bureau of Construction and Repair three new proposals which more closely met its stated criteria. The characteristics of this new design included a flushdeck hull of about 2050 tons displacement mounting five 5in/38 dual purpose guns, a single 1.1in AA weapon, and two quintuple 21in torpedo tubes.

From this initial design, the classic *Fletcher* class destroyer emerged. Early examples retained the rounded bridge structure of the earlier *Benson* class. While this arrangement was suitable for ships whose primary mission was torpedo attack, it soon became apparent that it was not suited to the increasing demands placed on the destroyer type to provide anti-aircraft protection for the proposed fast carriers. Accordingly, a new bridge was designed with angular sides and an open bridge completely around the enclosed bridge structure, at once simplifying construction and increasing air defense capability. At the same time, in order to increase stability and provide for the inevitable increases in topside weight that would come from the demand for additional anti-aircraft weapons and electronics, the foundation for the Mk 37 director was lowered about six feet. The result was the 'square bridge' *Fletcher*, the first of which was *Brownson* (DD 518). It was to this initial batch of 'square bridge' units that *The Sullivans* belonged.

SERVICE HISTORY

Maritime tradition holds that it is bad luck to change the name of a ship. Such does not seem to have been the case for *The Sullivans*, although her namesakes' luck tragically (and ironically) ran out on Friday, 13 November 1942. Originally slated to receive the name *Putnam*, DD 537 was renamed *The Sullivans* on 6 February 1943 to honor the memory of the five Sullivan brothers (Joseph, Francis, Albert, Madison, and George) who were lost when the light cruiser *Juneau* (CL 52) succumbed to Japanese torpedoes on that fateful Friday.

Built at Bethlehem's San Francisco yard, *The Sullivans* was launched 4 April 1943, christened by Mrs Thomas Sullivan, mother of the five brothers. Commissioning occurred on 30 September 1943, Commander Kenneth Gentry assuming command. Following shakedown, *The Sullivans* deployed to the Pacific, arriving at Pearl Harbor 28 December 1943. For the next eighteen

TABLE 1: **PARTICULARS OF USS THE SULLIVANS (DD 537)**

Class:		*Fletcher* (DD 445), modified
Length overall:		376ft 6in
Length on waterline:		369ft 0in
Beam:		39ft 8in
Draft:		13ft 5in
Displacement:		2150 long tons (standard)
Shaft horsepower:		60,000
Speed:		35kts (trial)
Range:		4900nm at 12kts (varies with load)
Armament:	(1943)	5 – 5in/38 Mk 30
		5 – twin 40mm Mk 1
		7 – 20mm Mk 4
		2 – 21in quintuple torpedo tubes Mk 14 & Mk 15
		6 – Mk 6 depth charge projectors
		2 – Mk 3 depth charge racks
	(1945)	5 – 5in/38 Mk 30
		3 – Twin 40mm Mk 1
		2 – Quad 40mm Mk 2
		6 – 20mm Mk 24 twin mounts
		1 – 21in quintuple torpedo tube Mk 14
		6 – Mk 6 depth charge projectors
		2 – Mk 3 depth charge racks
	(1959)	4 – 5in/38 Mk 30
		3 – Twin 3in/50 Mk 27
		2 – Mk 10 7.2in ASW projectors
		2 – Mk 3 depth charge racks
		1 – 21in quintuple torpedo tube Mk 14

months, *The Sullivans* was actively engaged in operations ranging from plane guard for the fast carriers to shore bombardment to anti-Kamikaze picket duty off Okinawa. There were occasional lulls in this schedule for routine maintenance and repair of battle damage, including some caused when she was swept against the battleship *Massachusetts* during a replenishment evolution at Saipan. A lucky ship, *The Sullivans* came through the devastating typhoon of 18 December 1944 that cost the Third Fleet three destroyers and scores of men.

The Sullivans' last combat action of World War II came on 14 May 1945, when she was screening *Enterprise* (CV 6). Having spent most of her time screening the fast carriers from air attack, this came as a fitting end to her duties as she was able to knock down one of the four Japanese aircraft lost in that attack. Following this action, she received orders to Mare Island for an AA refit, arriving there on 9 July. Not long after this overhaul, she was decommissioned and placed in reserve, where she remained from January 1946 until May 1951.

Once again, the winds of war blew and *The Sullivans* deployed to the Pacific, arriving at Sasebo, Japan on 10 October 1952. Assigned to Task Force 77 off Korea, she provided screening for the carriers and shore bombardment support for the UN ground forces, her favorite targets being railroad tunnels, bridges, and rolling stock.

Returning to the US in April 1953, she alternated between East Coast operations and deployments to the Mediterranean. In 1958, *The Sullivans* supported the Marine landings in Beirut, Lebanon, returning to the US for another period in the yard. On 5 May 1961, she provided support for the *Lake Champlain* (CVS 39) during a Mercury Project spaceshot and, seventeen months later, was involved in the blockade of Cuba during the October Missile Crisis.

Assigned to the Naval Reserve training force in April 1964, she continued her training duties until 7 January 1965 when she was decommissioned for the last time and laid up at the Philadelphia Naval Shipyard. There she languished until 1977, when she was acquired by the city of Buffalo, NY and, along with the cruiser *Little Rock*, was placed on display as a museum ship.

As of this writing (1987), *The Sullivans* remains a museum ship at Buffalo. Although she is much modified from her original WWII appearance, she is still easily recognizable as a 'square-bridge' *Fletcher* and provides an interesting contrast to the other two restored *Fletcher*s (*Kidd* at Baton Rouge, Louisiana and *Cassin Young* at Boston, Massachusetts), both of which have retained most of their original configuration.

CAREER SUMMARY
10 October 1942:   Laid down as *Putnam*
6 February 1943:   Name changed to *The Sullivans*
4 April 1943:   Launched, Mrs T F Sullivan sponsoring
30 September 1943:   Commissioned, Cdr K M Gentry commanding
28 December 1943:   Arrived Pearl Harbor and assigned to TG 58.2
24 January – 21 February 1944:   Screened TG 58.2 bombardment of Truk
29 April 1944:   Shot down first aircraft while screening airstrikes on Truk
1 May 1944:   Bombarded Ponape
6–19 June 1944:   Screened airstrikes on Saipan
4 July 1944:   Bombarded coast of Iwo Jima, destroying five G4M2 ('Betty') aircraft in revetments
28 September 1944:   Damaged by being swept into USS *Massachusetts* (BB 59)
6–18 October 1944:   Screened airstrikes against Formosa. Rescued 118 men from *Houston* (CL 81) following torpedo attack
18 December 1944:   Survived typhoon
14–25 March 1945:   Screened airstrikes on Honshu. Provided assistance to *Halsey Powell* (DD 686) following Kamikaze attack
15 April – 30 May 1945:   Anti-Kamikaze picket duty off Okinawa. Rescued 166 survivors of *Bunker Hill* (CV 13)
14 May 1945:   Final action of World War II – shot down one aircraft while assisting *Enterprise* (CV 6)
9 July 1945:   Arrived Mare Island for AA overhaul
10 January 1946:   Decommissioned at San Diego, CA
6 July 1951:   Recommissioned

11–20 October 1952:   Screened airstrikes on Korea for TF 77
14 December 1952 – early January 1953:   Bombarded railroad tunnels, bridges, and rolling stock in the Songjin area
26 January 1953:   Departed Yokosuka for US
April 1954 – December 1960:   Alternated between East Coast operations and Mediterranean deployments including support of 1958 landings in Beirut
5 May 1961:   Participated in Project Mercury retrieval of Cdr Allan Shepard
September 1961 – February 1962:   Major overhaul at Boston
October 1962:   Engaged in blockade of Cuba during the 'Missile Crisis'
1 April 1964:   Transferred to Naval Reserve
7 January 1965:   Decommissioned at Philadelphia

GENERAL ARRANGEMENT AND HULL STRUCTURE
Of all-welded construction, *The Sullivans'* graceful hull was a flush-deck design incorporating both longitudinal and transverse framing. Watertight integrity was enhanced by 14 water-tight bulkheads, pierced by water-tight hatches only on the first platform deck level. Below the first platform level, access to all water-tight compartments was limited to water-tight scuttles fitted to the decks above. Further protection was provided by seven oil-tight bulkheads.

The engineering spaces were staggered to enhance powerplant survivability and were arranged fire room, engine room, fire room, engine room. The forward pair serviced the starboard shaft; the after pair, the port shaft. The engineering spaces could be reached only from the main deck. Fuel oil was stored in compartments forward and aft of the engineering spaces below the second platform deck and reserve feedwater and freshwater tanks were fitted outboard of both fire rooms.

Enlisted crew were accommodated on the second platform deck forward and the first platform deck aft, with washrooms and heads located in the after deckhouse on the main deck. The messdeck and scullery were located on the second platform deck forward. CPOs and ship's officers shared the first platform deck forward. The wardroom was located on the main deck level in the forward superstructure.

Workshops were generally restricted to the first platform deck, although the superstructure amidships contained the galley, torpedo ordnance workshop, and laundry. Stores were distributed throughout the second and third platform decks, and the hold.

On the superstructure deck level, the bridge contained radio central and a 40mm clipping room, the latter being converted to a 7.2in projectile room during the 1959 refit. At the navigating bridge level, the bridge contained the pilot house, fire control station, and sonar room.

Structurally, *The Sullivans'* hull followed standard construction practices for welded units. The details of the principal structural features were:
Keel: The keel was a single 21in × 8¼in I-beam running the length of the ship. Bilge keels were fitted just above longitudinal No 7 extending the length of the engineering spaces.
Longitudinal frames: Longitudinal frames were fitted the full length of the hull and deck on *The Sullivans*. Sixteen longitudinals ran along either side of the keel up to the main deck level. These longitudinals were generally either 10in × 4in or 6in × 4in T-sections cut from larer I-beams. Fifteen T-section longitudinals supported the main deck, these being either 12in × 4in or 9.9in × 5.75in members.
Transverse frames: Transverse framing in *The Sullivans* consisted of 210 frames, 14 of which were water-tight bulkheads, seven of which were oil-tight

bulkheads, and the remainder web frames. Frame spacing was 21in.

Decks: *The Sullivans'* hull incorporated three primary decks (main, first, and second platform), and a half deck (third platform), while the hold and engineering spaces were provided with flats where necessary. Of the primary decks, only the main deck was continuous. The first platform deck was interrupted by the engineering spaces between frames 72 and 157, the second platform deck between frames 60 and 157, while the third platform deck terminated at frame 42. All decks were fitted with water-tight scuttles and vertical or inclined ladders for access. Main deck plating was generally 20# STS, while the lower decks made do with 7.65# STS.

Shell plating: There were seven strakes on either side of the keel. Starting at the main deck, there were two of 30# STS, followed by two of 12# HTS, one of 15# HTS, one of 18# HTS, and one of 20# HTS. A garboard strake of 25# HTS covered the keel.

MACHINERY ARRANGEMENTS – MAIN STEAM SYSTEM

The Sullivans' engineering plant consisted of a forward and after machinery system. Each system comprised two boilers which provided steam for a turbine and double reduction gear unit driving a propeller shaft. Condensing equipment and other necessary auxiliaries were also provided.

The forward and after systems were arranged to operate independently or could be cross-connected for operating flexibility in restricted waters or in an emergency. Split plant operation was the normal operating procedure and was required in combat to prevent loss of the entire machinery system due to damage at a single point in the system. As a rule, the forward engine room functioned as the control room.

Boilers: The boilers were of the divided-furnace, single-uptake, three-drum express type with integral separately-fired superheater, economizer, and soot blowers. The open fire room system was employed. The boilers were equipped with double air casing, the inner and outer casings forming a duct through which air from the forced draft blowers flowed around the boiler to the registers at the front of the furnace.

Superheat: Superheated steam was used for extended cruising at speeds in excess of 12 knots. This was an important factor affecting fuel economy and cruising radius, and was essential to the development of the full designed horsepower. With the ship operating under the ahead condition, designed steam conditions at the superheater outlet were 565psi (pounds per square inch), at temperatures not exceeding 850°F. When going astern, the temperature was reduced to approximately 700°F.

Main steam piping: The main steam piping system supplied steam to the main propulsion turbines, turbo-generators, and the soot blowers.

Saturated steam from the steam drum passed through the superheater and from the superheater outlet to the main steam lines. Each boiler was provided with a boiler stop valve, operable from the main deck or from the fire room, and the line from each boiler was fitted with a bulkhead stop valve in the engine room, providing two-valve protection for a boiler not in use. This arrangement also provided effective isolation in case of damage. These valves were always open when the boiler was on line and fully shut when the unit was secured.

The main steam lines from the two boilers in each fire room were combined in the corresponding engine room, forming a single line which led to the main steam strainer through an automatic overspeed control valve to the cam-operated nozzle valves of the high-pressure or cruising turbine, both of which were controlled from the main gauge board. For astern operation, the steam passed from the strainer via the astern throttle valve to the astern steam chest.

The turbo-generators were fitted with a connection from the main steam line directly ahead of the main steam strainer, and also with a connection from the saturated auxiliary steam line. Turbo-generators were operated from the main steam lines whenever conditions permitted. The shift from main to auxiliary, or vice versa, was made slowly to guard against loss of electrical load due to carry-over of condensation from the line into the turbine.

The forward and after main steam systems were connected by the cross-connection piping in the forward engine room. This line was provided with one stop valve in the forward engine room and another at the forward bulkhead of the after fire room. During split plant operation, these valves were both closed and the line drained.

Soot blowers: Soot-blower steam for cleaning soot from the generating tube banks, superheater, and economizer was taken from the superheater outlet piping directly ahead of the boiler stop valve. The soot-blower steam header formed a loop from which branches were taken to the individual blowers, each branch line being provided with a drain valve. The loop was drained to the bilge through a single valve.

Soot blowers were operated only when the boiler involved was being fired at a rate sufficient to prevent the fires from being blown out. Before blowing, the air pressure was increased to ensure that the loosened soot was carried out of the stack and to guard against flareback.

Main turbine steam flow: Each set of main propulsion turbines consisted of a cross-compound unit of cruising turbine, high-pressure turbine, and low-pressure turbine, the latter containing an astern element.

In operation, the main turbines could be divided into two distinct ahead conditions: cruising combination and high-pressure combination. In *cruising combination*, the steam flow from the main steam strainer was through the overspeed control valve to the cruising turbine throttle. The steam was used in the cruising turbine, exhausting through the 6in crossover valve to the first stage of the high-pressure turbine, flowing through the high-pressure turbine, high-pressure/low-pressure crossover, and through the low-pressure turbine to the condenser. This combination was normally used in the cruising range (up to 191rpm) for economy. In *high-pressure combination*, the steam flow from the main steam strainer was through the overspeed control valve to the high-pressure turbine throttle. The steam was used in the high-pressure crossover, and through the low-pressure turbine to the condenser. The cruising turbine control valves were shut, the cruising turbine connected through the 3½in crossover valve directly to the condenser, and a small flow of steam from the first stage of the high-pressure turbine was admitted to the cruising turbine for cooling the revolving rotor. This combination was used normally in the high-speed range and could be used in the cruising-speed range for greater maneuverability, but with resulting greater fuel consumption and reducing cruising radius.

For astern operation, the cruising and high-pressure turbine throttles were shut and the steam flow from the main strainer was through the astern throttle to the astern blading of the low-pressure turbine. The turbine exhausted to the main condenser. When going astern, the steam temperature was reduced to 675°F at the throttle.

Turbine drains: When warming up or securing the turbines, steam condensed and collected at low points in the turbine casings. Suitable turbine drains, fitted with stop valves or impulse traps, were provided to drain this condensate to the main condenser. The high-pressure and cruising turbine steam chests were drained to the condenser through combined strainer and impulse traps which were provided with manually-operated bypass valves controlled from the main gauge board. All other drains were controlled by stop valves with operating gear to the turbine platform. No external drain connections were required for the low-pressure turbine, as this unit drained directly to the condenser.

AUXILIARY STEAM SYSTEM

The auxiliary steam system supplied the steam-operated auxiliary equipment and heating services. Reducing valves were provided for such services as required steam at less than boiler pressure. Relief valves, set at slightly above the reduced pressure, protected the equipment and piping from excess pressure.

Saturated steam at 615psi was led from each boiler steam drum outlet through a stop valve and a guarding valve, the first of which was controlled from the deck, and was supplied to the full pressure auxiliary steam loop system. The system divided into a port and starboard line running the length of the machinery spaces. The two lines were interconnected in each of the engine and fire rooms and fitted with stop valves at each bulkhead, permitting flexibility of operation and providing for isolation of portions of the system in case of damage. Under normal conditions, both the port and starboard lines were in service and the engine room interconnecting valves were closed.

One boiler could supply the auxiliary steam required to operate the necessary auxiliaries and equipment in the entire ship for warming up and standing by, including one turbo-generator and the ship's service steam. The auxiliaries and services operating on the full pressure auxiliary steam loop were:

- forced draft blowers
- fuel-oil service pumps
- fuel-oil booster pumps
- high-pressure air compressor
- main feed pumps
- main feed booster pumps (turbine-driven)
- emergency feed pumps
- fire and bilge pumps
- main condenser circulating pumps
- main condensate pumps (turbine-driven)
- main lubricating oil pumps (turbine-driven)
- turbo-generators
- fuel oil heaters
- steam smothering system (overhead)

Branch lines to auxiliaries were provided with root valves to permit isolation of the branch in case of damage or for throttle or governor valve repair.

The piping to the two forced-draft blowers serving each boiler were arranged to permit operation of either blower individually or the two in parallel. A root valve controlling flow of steam to both blowers, with gear for operation from platform or firing aisle, was located at the boiler front. A needle valve was installed in the branch line to each blower for individual operation. The branch lines were designed to provide substantially equal chest pressures and speeds on the two blowers when both were in operation. Any compensation required in paralleling could be made by the needle valves.

Smothering steam lines were located well overhead, near the main deck, in each of the machinery spaces. This location enabled the system to deal effectively with an oil fire in a flooded compartment. The control valves for steam smothering were operated from the main deck near the escape hatch.

The fuel-oil heater group in each fire room was provided with a needle valve for control and regulation, and a stop valve bypass for alternative operation.

Each individual heater element was fitted with a cutout valve after these control valves.

Reduced-pressure auxiliary steam: Reduced-pressure auxiliary steam was provided to a variety of units at varying levels of pressure. The major levels and their associated equipment were:

275psi – supplied to the main and auxiliary air ejectors through reducing valves from the 615psi auxiliary steam line.

165psi – supplied for various services through reducing valves from the 615psi auxiliary steam line. Two reducing valves were provided aft of the after boiler in each fire room. Each valve was capable of supplying the full normal requirements of the 165psi services, so no bypasses were fitted. 165psi steam supplied the following services:

- distilling plant air ejectors
- whistle and siren
- heating coils – fuel-oil tanks and lubricating-oil storage tanks
- hose connections in machinery spaces for blowing out sea chests and scoops, for cleaning burner atomizer tips, and for boiler boiling-out
- bilge smothering and boiler casing steam smothering
- depth charge de-icing

100psi – supplied steam to the laundry and pressing room through a 165–100psi reducing valve in the forward engine room

45psi – supplied through a reducing valve from the 165psi line for the following services:

- heaters for lubricating-oil purifying system
- steam heating system
- constant steam system (galley, hot water, etc.)

10psi – supplied steam through a special 45–10psi valve from the steam heating line in the after fire room to the torpedo tubes for heating

Shore heating: Shore steam was supplied from either side of the ship through a hose connection and valve on the main deck to the 165psi line in the forward fire room for the operation of the 165psi services. Shore steam was lead through a stop-check valve from the 165psi line in either fire room to the full-pressure auxiliary steam main. This connection permitted operation of fuel-oil heaters and auxiliary machinery required for cold starting or of smothering steam for emergency use in port.

AUXILIARY EXHAUST SYSTEM

The auxiliary exhaust system collected exhaust steam from all steam-driven auxiliary machinery and supplied it to the gland sealing system, distilling plant, and, primarily, to the deaerating feed tank for feed heating. The forward and after machinery groups could be operated independently or cross-connected.

The system operated at a nominal pressure of 15psi and was designed for fully automatic control. If the exhaust was insufficient to heat the feed to the desired temperature, it was augmented by bleeder steam or by steam taken from the 165psi steam line through automatic pressure-regulating valves. Excess auxiliary exhaust could be unloaded to either the main condenser or the auxiliary condenser through automatic unloading valves.

Exhaust casings of all turbine-driven auxiliaries were protected against excess pressure by exhaust valves of the spring-loaded type and by relief valves set at 25psi. A sentinel valve set at 23psi was also provided on the exhaust line near each deaerating tank. Exhaust pressure could be relieved to the atmospheric escape pipe in an emergency through a spring-loaded atmospheric exhaust valve located in each fire room.

STEAM DRAIN COLLECTING SYSTEM

The steam drain collecting system consisted of three principal drain mains:

- high pressure
- low pressure
- inspection tank

These mains extended throughout the machinery spaces and could be arranged for cross-connection or split plant operation. The high- and low-presure mains were provided with stop valves at each bulkhead for damage isolation.

High-pressure drains: The high-pressure drain mains collected all drains from the main steam and full pressure and 165psi auxiliary steam piping, steam separators, and boiler superheaters through combined strainers and impulse traps and discharged them to the deaerating feed tanks. Each of these drains was also provided with atmospheric discharges to the low-pressure drain main or to the bilge under conditions where the pressure is insufficient to deliver to the deaerating tank. The system was designed to operate at 35psi and was protected by relief valves set at 40psi.

Low-pressure drains: The low-pressure drain main collected all low-pressure drains, including drains from reduced pressure (except 165psi) auxiliary steam piping, various auxiliary equipment, and heating system returns, except those which could be contaminated by oil leakage, and discharged them to the fresh water drain tanks. The drain inlet to each tank was equipped with a stop valve, permitting disposal of all drains to one tank if required by operating conditions or damage.

Inspection tank drains: Drains from the fuel-oil heaters, fuel-oil tank heating coils, and lubricating-oil storage tank heating coils were led to the inspection tank drain main, which discharged to an inspection tank in each engine room. The inspection tank normally discharged into the deaerating feed tank, although it could discharge to the low-pressure drain main.

MAIN FEED AND CONDENSATE SYSTEM

The feed system was of the fully-enclosed type, which involved the following features:

- all condensate lines were under positive pressure except the short line from condenser hotwell to condensate pump suction
- feed water had no contact with atmospheric air at any point from condenser to boiler
- all condensate, including drains and makeup, was heated to feed temperature and deaerated by direct contact with auxiliary exhaust steam in the deaerating feed tank before passing to the boilers

There were two complete feed systems, forward and aft, which were normally operated as completely separate and independent units (split-plant). Split plant operation was required under combat conditions or in an emergency to guard against derangement of the entire machinery plant due to a single hit at any point of the feed system.

Normal operating cycle: Condensate from the main condenser hotwell was pumped by the main condensate pump through the inter and after condenser of the main air ejector and the deaerating feed heater vent condenser into the deaerating tank. Condensate from the auxiliary condenser hotwell was pumped by the auxiliary condensate pump through the inter and after condenser of the auxiliary air ejector, entering the main condensate line ahead of the deaerating feed tank vent condenser. After heating and deaerating, the feed was taken from the bottom of the deaerating tank shell by the feed booster pumps and delivered to the main or emergency feed pump suction at sufficient pressure to prevent flashing. The feed pumps discharged the feed through economizers into the boilers at a normal operating pressure of 750psi at 245°F. Control of the rate of feed was accomplished manually through the boiler feed stop-check valves or automatically by Bailey Feedwater Regulators.

Deaerating feed tank: The deaerating feed tank was the key to successful operation of the feed system, performing the functions of feed heating, deaerating, hotwater storage, and surge provision. Condensate entered the tank through the vent condenser and passed to a spray head from which it was sprayed through nozzles into the surrounding atmosphere of steam in the upper heating section. The heated condensate fell toward the steam atomizing valve where the entering steam divided the water into fine particles, liberating entrained gases and dissolved oxygen and sweeping them out of the tank via the vent condenser unit.

The non-condensable gases, with a small quantity of uncondensed water vapor, were vented to the auxiliary condenser or the after condenser of the main air ejector. The atomizing valve, when set for automatic operation, admitted the required amount of steam for heating and deaeration, and maintained the deaerating tank pressure at approximately 1psi below the auxiliary exhaust line pressure.

Reserve feed: There were two reserve feed tanks in each fire room which could supply make-up feed to the main or auxiliary condensers by vacuum drag, or could receive excess feed from the condensate discharge line. Transfer of reserve feed between tanks was accomplished by means of the emergency feed pump.

Emergency feed pump: Emergency feed pumps were employed for port and at-anchor service at low steaming rates, and for emergency service. The pumps could take suction from the booster pumps in either engine room, to deliver hot feed to either fire room. The emergency feed pumps were employed for transferring feed as well as supplying feed to the boilers.

FUEL-OIL SERVICE SYSTEM

The fuel-oil service system was designed to deliver fuel oil to the boilers at suitable pressure and temperature for proper atomization and combustion in the furnaces. The systems in each fire room were arranged for independent operation.

Two service tanks supplied fuel oil to each fire room through deck-operated valves located at the tank bulkheads. The fuel-oil service pumps were arranged to take suction from the high suction of either service tank, or from the fuel-oil booster discharge through the fuel-oil transfer main. The service pumps discharged through a meter, fuel-oil heaters, and a duplex strainer to the boilers. The meter and heaters were provided with a cutout and bypass valves in case of damage, leakage, or clogging. The fuel-oil main divided at the firing aisle into branches serving each boiler, each being provided with a stop valve and a quick-closing gate valve for emergencies. Micrometer valves were installed in the piping to the saturated and superheat burner manifolds for close adjustment of the fuel-oil supply. The manifolds delivered oil to the individual burners.

The main fuel-oil service pumps were capable of delivering fuel-oil at a pressure of 350psi and were protected by relief valves set at 355psi. Either pump was capable of supplying both boilers at the maximum combustion rate.

Each fire room was equipped with four fuel-oil heaters, connected in parallel and provided with separate cutout valves. The number of heaters used depended on the rate of firing and as sufficient to heat the oil to the correct temperature for proper atomization.

Provision was made for recirculation from the burner manifolds back to the fuel-oil service pump suction during lighting-off periods by valves. During normal operation, these valves were closed.

MAIN LUBRICATING-OIL SYSTEM
The main lubricating-oil system delivered lubricating oil under forced feed to the main turbine journal and thrust bearings, the main reduction gear sprays, and reduction gear bearings. There were two rotary pumps for each engine room, rated at 600gpm (gallons per minute) with a discharge pressure of 35psi. These pumps were either motor-driven or turbine-driven and could supply full-power operation requirements singly. Relief valves on turbine-driven pumps were set at 45psi, while those on motor-driven pumps were set at 50psi.

In operation, the lubricating-oil pumps took suction through a common line from the main lubricating drain tank, discharging through lift-check and gate valves, duplex strainer, and lubricating-oil coolers to a main supply header. Lines from the main supply header delivered oil to the reduction gear sprays, gear bearings, and turbine journal and thrust bearings.

MAIN AND CRUISING REDUCTION GEARS
The gear units for port and starboard drives were alike in all major features, except that they were opposite hand. The gearing itself was of the double opposed-helix type.

Main reduction unit: The main reduction unit comprised two sets of gears with a common low-speed element. One set was for the high-pressure turbine drive and the other for the low-pressure turbine drive. Both were contained in a single casing which also housed the propeller thrust bearing and which formed the mounting for the turning gear.

Each set of gears consisted of a high-speed pinion, two intermediate-speed gears, two intermediate-speed pinions, and the common low-speed gear. All pinions were completely machined out of specially heat-treated nickel steel forgings. The gear wheels were of built-up construction with teeth cut in seamless steel bands which were welded to fabricated steel spiders. In the low-speed rotor, the gear wheel was pressed on the shaft against a locating-shaft shoulder and secured by two keys and a locknut. The intermediate-speed gear wheels were shrunk and welded on their respective shafts.

The casing was of welded steel construction and was divided into four main parts:
- base section, which mounts the low-speed rotor
- intermediate section, which carries the high-speed pinions, intermediate-speed gears and pinions
- two main cover sections

All-metal flexible couplings were used to connect the high-speed pinions and the turbine shafts, as well as for the connections between the intermediate-speed gears and pinions. The coupling between the low-speed rotor and the propeller shafting was of the rigid type in which flanges formed on the shaft ends were connected by fitted bolts.

Cruising reduction unit: The cruising unit had only one pinion and one gear. The pinion was coupled rigidly to the shaft of the cruising turbine, while the gear was connected to the high-pressure turbine by a flexible coupling. The pinion and the gear were carried in babbitt-lined, split-sleeve bearings and were housed in a horizontally-split, cast-steel casing. Both rotors were machined completely out of solid-steel forgings.

Flexible couplings: All flexible couplings were of the enclosed gear type in which a floating intermediate gear element meshes completely with teeth on the ends of the driving and driven shafts.

The couplings between the main turbines and the high-speed pinions were floating members which took the form of a hollow shaft with teeth at each end which meshed completely with the internal teeth of rings bolted to the flanged ends of the connected shafts.

The intermediate-speed gears and pinions were connected by a quill shaft running through the shafts of the intermediate-speed gear and pinion rotors, which meshed with the teeth of rings bolted to the flanged ends of the driving and driven shafts.

In the cruising-gear unit, the floating member was a vertically-split sleeve having internal teeth which meshed completely with the external teeth of spur gears mounted on the connected shaft ends.

Propeller thrust bearing: This component was a 28in Kingsbury thrust bearing built into the main reduction-gear unit at the forward end of the low-speed gear shaft. It consisted of a steel rotating element, two sets of stationary pivoted babbitt-faced bronze segments and a load-equalizing mounting for each set of shoes.

Turning gear: The turning gear unit was mounted on the after end of the main gear casing, in line with the high-pressure, high-speed pinion. It consisted of an electric motor, two sets of worm gears, and a set of spur gears. The motor was connected to the high-speed worm by a flexible coupling of the rubber-bushed pin type. A manually-operated jaw-type clutch, which was built into the low-speed turning gear element, formed the conection between the turning gear unit and the main pinion when the turning gear was in use.

The motor was a Westinghouse 5hp, 440-volt, 3-phase, 60-cycle, 1800rpm synchronous speed, 1700rpm full-load speed, induction motor equipped with a Westinghouse across-the-line, reversing type, magnetic starter with push-button control.

Speed ratios for the reduction gears were:
- first reduction   17.5 : 1
- second reduction   17.5 : 1
- third reduction   3.4375 : 1
- overall   1053 : 1

The ratio of turning-gear motor speed to propeller speed was 15,088 : 1.

CONDENSING EQUIPMENT
The primary condensing equipment aboard *The Sullivans* was built by the Foster Wheeler Corporation and consisted of two each of the following:
- main condensers
- auxiliary condensers
- main ejectors
- auxiliary ejectors

The main condensers were single-pass units containing 11,000sq ft of surface each. Non-condensable vapors from each main condenser were discharged into a two-stage, twin-element steam jet air ejector with surface-type inter and after condenser that included a gland steam condenser in the same shell. The auxiliary condensers were of the two-pass type containing 580sq ft of surface in each unit. Non-condensable vapors were removed from each auxiliary condenser by a two-stage, twin-element steam jet air ejector with surface inter and after condenser.

Main condenser: The main condenser was located directly below the low-pressure turbine and was supported by the turbine exhaust flange to which it was bolted by 112 steel bolts one inch in diameter.

The main condenser was designed with a shallow tube bank which permitted a low center of gravity and high heat transfer efficiency. The tubes were placed in four groups with steam lanes between the groups to give a large entrance area into tube banks and to permit heating the condensate close to steam temperature. Each of the four tube groups had its own air cooler section which was partitioned off from the condensing tubes by a double baffle which also acted as a condensate collecting plate. Condensate which collected above the air baffle was piped to receiving trays immediately below the tubes. The two trays on each side of the condenser discharged their contents to a heating tray in the space between them. The condensate was exposed to exhaust steam which had a free access to the heating tray through the lane between the two groups of tubes. The condensate then flowed through a series of small holes into the condenser hotwell. The lower portion of the condenser was baffled throughout its length to prevent surging of condensate from one end to the other or from side to side when the ship pitched or rolled.

Main air ejectors: Each main air ejector was of two-stage, twin-element type with common surface-type inter and after condensers. In the same shell with the inter and after condenser, and using the same circulating water system, was the gland steam condenser which served the main turbine. Each ejector element was equipped with isolating valves to permit removal of the element without shutting down the entire air ejector and to permit operation with only one set of elements when air leakage was not excessive.

Auxiliary condenser: The auxiliary condenser in each engine room was placed below the turbine room grating and was supported by two brackets bolted on the ship's framework. The condenser was arranged for two passes of water flow. The tubes were placed in two banks, all of the tubes being on conventional triangular spacing. Part of the tubes of the lower pass were baffled off to provide an air cooling section. The entire periphery of each tube bank was exposed to entering steam except for the small space provided for air offtake from the lower tube bank. The hotwell was likewise exposed to entering steam to provide maximum deaeration of condensate and minimum depression of condensate temperature.

Auxiliary air ejectors: Each auxiliary air ejector was similar to the main air ejectors, except that there was no gland steam condensing section and all were made to the same hand. Isolating valves were included and, in addition to the parts similar to those on the main air ejectors, there was also a complete set of steam piping.

TABLE 2: **PARTICULARS OF THE MAIN CONDENSERS**

Total weight of one condenser:	51,490lb
Weight of one inlet water chest:	3100lb
Weight of one discharge water chest:	2390lb
Total weight of one condenser with water space filled:	71,625lb
Total tube surface:	11,000sq ft
Surface in air cooling sections:	746sq ft
Surface in condensing sections:	10,254sq ft
Total number of tubes:	6404
Performance at full load:	
Steam flow to condenser:	210,000lb/hr
Water flow through condenser:	32,500gpm
Absolute pressure at top of condenser:	1.25psi
Water inlet temperature:	65°F
Water velocity through tubes:	7.5fps

GUN ARMAMENT

Like the preceding *Benson/Livermore* classes, *The Sullivans* carried the highly successful dual-purpose 5in/38 in single, shielded base-ring mounts. The basic mount was the Mk 30 and *The Sullivans* carried five of these on the centerline disposed as follows:

- Main deck – one Mod 18 or Mod 19 mount forward and aft
- Superstructure deck – one Mod 30 or Mod 31 mount forward and one on either end of the 40mm platform aft

The primary difference between the Mod 18/19 and the Mod 30/31 was the shape of the shield, the former having three segments to the roof, the latter only two. There were, of course, minor variations further distinguishing the various Mods. Generally, the Mod 18/19 mounts were fitted with a shield around the mount captain's hatch to protect him from the muzzle blast of the superfiring mounts. *The Sullivans*, however, carried the mount captain's shield on all but the forward superfiring mount, quite possibly because of the muzzle blast from the after 40mm mount.

The basic mount consisted of a single Mk 12 Mod 1 weapon enclosed in a 0.25in thick shield which was serviced by a handling room directly below the base ring. Integral to the mount were a powder hoist Mk 2 and a projectile hoist Mk 2, allowing the ammunition to be passed at any angle of train. The mount was power-driven, although in an emergency, it could be manually operated.

All mounts were equipped with electric–hydraulic power drives for training and elevating the gun, a single motor driving separate hydraulic transmision units. Each transmission unit consisted of a pump connected by pressure lines to a hydraulic motor and a control unit containing valves and control devices which regulated the output of the pump to the motor. Three modes of control were available:

- *Automatic* – control from a director system by means of electrical signals transmitted to the indicator–regulator which, in turn, controlled the output of the hydraulic pump
- *Local* – control of the power drive by means of pointer's and trainer's handwheels, the rotation of which replaced the electrical signals from the director. High and low speed could be selected using levers at the pointer's and trainer's stations.
- *Manual* – control by the handwheels geared directly to the training and elevating tracks. Only low speed was available in this mode

Under power, the training gear rate was about 29° per second, while elevation rate was about 15° per second. Elevation limits were minus 15° to plus 85°.

A dual-tube projectile hoist was fitted to each base-ring mount. The assembly consisted of a hoisting unit in two enclosed tubes, an electric–hydraulic power drive, and semi-automatic control equipment. The hoist was also equipped with a fuze-setting device which automatically set the fuzes as the projectiles were lifted from the handling room to the mount.

Long-range AA: The primary long-range anti-aircraft weapon on *The Sullivans* was the 40mm Bofors, in both twin and quadruple mounts. After World War II, this weapon was replaced with the twin 3in/50 automatic Mk 27 mount.

When commissioned in 1943, *The Sullivans* carried five twin Mk 1 mounts in the following arrangement:

- two mounts forward on the superstructure deck abaft mount 52
- two mounts abeam the aft stack on the superstructure deck level
- one mount on the centerline on a platform one deck level above the superstructure deck between mounts 53 and 54

By 1945, the need for augmented AA to counter the growing threat from

TABLE 3: PARTICULARS OF SHIP'S GUNS

5in/38 Mk 30

Type:	5in/38 Mk 12 Mod 1
Max. powder pressure:	18 long tons/sq in
Barrel weight:	3990lb
Mount weight:	45,000lb (approx)
Muzzle velocity:	2600fps
Max altitude:	37,200ft at 85° elevation
Max range:	18,200yds at 45°10' elevation
Ammunition (separate case):	Projectile types
	AA projectile Mk 35, 55.2lb
	Common projectile Mk 32, 54.0lb
	Illuminating projectile Mk 30, 54.5lb
	Cartridge
	Case Mk 5 Mod 0, 12.3lb
	Charge nominal 15.2lb
	Primer Mk 13 Mod 0
Trunnion pressure:	Horizontal fire 78,900lb
	85° elevation fire 91,500lb

3in/50 Mk 27

Type:	3in/50 Mk 22 Mod 4 throught Mod 9
Max powder pressure:	17 long tons/sq in
Weight per gun:	1242lb
Mount weight:	34,750lb
Off mount equipment:	3350lb
Muzzle velocity:	2700fps
Max altitude:	30,400ft
Max range:	14,200yds
Operating characteristics:	Training 30°/sec; 360°
	Elevation 24°/sec; +85°, −15°
Ammunition (fixed case):	Projectile types
	AA Mk 27, 13.05lb
	AP Mk 29, 13.07lb
	Illuminating Mk 25, 13.07lb
	Case
	Mk 7, powder charge 4lb, total wt 7lb
	Mk 9, powder charge 4lb, total wt 6.5lb

40mm Mk 1 – twin

Type:	40mm/60 Mk 1 Mods 1 through 3
Max powder pressure:	19.5 long tons/sq in
Barrel weight:	202lb/gun
Mount weight:	14,900lb/power driven
Muzzle velocity:	2890fps
Cyclic:	160rpm
Max altitude:	22,800ft at 90°
Max range:	11,000yds at 42°
Ammunition (fixed):	Projectile type
	AA, AP, 1.98lb/projectile
	4.75lb/round
	20lb/clip
	Case
	Mk 1 Mod 0, 1.89lb
	Mk 2 Mod 0, 1.93lb
	Mk 3 Mod 0, 1.53lb

40mm Mk 2 – quad

Characteristics as for Mk 1 except for:

Mount weight:	26,600lb

20mm Mk 4

Type:	20mm/70 Mk 4 Mod 0 or 1
Max powder pressure:	None set
Barrel and mechanism weight:	150lb
Cyclic:	450rpm
Ballistics:	HE
	Projectile Mk 3, 0.2714lb
	Case Mk 2, 0.190lb
	Charge 27.7grams
	Primer Mk 90
	APT
	Projectile Mk 9, 0.2686lb
	Case Mk 3, 0.180lb
	Charge 27.7grams
Mount weight:	1685lb
Shield:	250lb
Brake load:	1785lb

20mm Mk 24 – twin

Type:	20mm/70 Mk 4 Mod 0 or 1
Barrel and mechanism weight:	150lb/gun
Cyclic:	450rpm
Muzzle velocity:	2740fps
Max altitude:	10,000ft at 90°
Max range:	4800yds at 35°
Ammunition:	as for Mk 4
Mount weight:	1400lb
Shield:	250lb
Brake load:	3570lb

Both the twin and quad mounts were power-driven, water-cooled units having both local and automatic control, the latter being provided by the versatile Mk 51 director and its associated Mk 14 gunsight. By the end of the war, the quad mounts would be controlled by the Mk 63 director, its radar dish being mounted directly on the gun itself. Under power operation, training rate was 30° per second. Elevation limits were minus 15° to plus 90°, with an elevation rate of 24° per second.

The weapon was a recoil-operated heavy machine gun designed primarily for anti-aircraft fire. Its distinctive features included a liquid-cooled barrel, vertical sliding-wedge breech mechanism, hand-fed automatic loader, and spring-operated rammer. The trigger mechanism controlled the rammer operation only; once the ramming cycle started, the round was loaded and fired automatically without further control. The gun could be set for single or automatic fire, the firing rate in automatic being about 120 rpm.

Post-war, all 40mm mounts were replaced by the twin 3in/50 Mk 27. These were mounted in the same positions as the 1945 40mm battery; in fact, the mount was designed to use the same base ring. Each mount had high-speed power drive gun-laying equipment, but could not be trained manually. Gun-laying controls included selective remote and local facilities, the local control units being duplicate stations on either wing of the platform. Pedestal design and the arrangement of the slides and elevating gear gave a total gun-laying movement of 100 degrees and permitted loading and firing throughout the arc. Between the two pedestals, a transverse beam braced the structure and provided bracket mounting for equipment of a central gun-loading control station.

The platform on which the two gun pedestals were mounted was a welded rectangular structure on which were mounted all other parts of the mount. It had wing extensions and floor plates providing working areas for the crew. The structure was secured to a lower base ring which was supported on roller bearings. A meshing pinion and train power drive turned the carriage;

Kamikaze attacks was evident and, during her AA refit in the summer of 1945, *The Sullivans* had the twin mounts abeam the aft stack replaced with a pair of quad Mk 2 mounts. These weapons, and their associated tower for the Mk 63 directors, were mounted between the stacks, necessitating the removal of the forward Mk 14 torpedo tubes.

elevation was through a power-driven cross shaft connecting separate elevating pinions and arc mechanisms. Power systems were electrical amplidyne systems and were arranged for local control at either of the one-man control units. Four rotating-drum ready service magazines were fitted to the rear of the stand, each capable of holding six rounds.

Short range AA: The primary short range anti-aircraft weapon aboard *The Sullivans* was the 20mm Oerlikon. Initially, *The Sullivans* carried seven single Mk 4 mounts, two on each beam on the main deck level just aft of the waist 40mm mounts and three in a triangular shield on the fantail. During her 1945 AA refit, these mounts were replaced by six twin Mk 24 mounts which occupied essentially the same positions.

The Mk 4 mount featured a cast pedestal and a variable height cradle. The pedestal was bolted to the deck but the pedestal head, through which the column rose, rotated around the top of the pedestal and could be locked in any position by a clamping lever. The column could be raised about 15 inches by a handwheel on the head, giving the gunner a better position for high-angle fire. Mounted on top of the column were the trunnion bracket and pivot, which also provided support for the shield, cradle spiral spring, and cradle, to which the gun was bolted. The cradle spring, mounted around the left trunnion, had one end attached to the trunnion and the other to the spring case, thus acting as a counterbalance to the weight of the gun.

The Mk 24 mount, on the other hand, featured a lighter tripod and a fixed trunnion height, although the other major components were similar to the Mk 4. To compensate for the loss of trunnion adjustment, the Mk 24 mount was somewhat higher and had a circular stepped platform attached to the bottom of the tripod for the gunner to stand on.

The gun was a 20mm, 70 caliber weapon consisting of four main groups:
- barrel and breech casing
- breechblock
- recoil and counterrecoil system
- trigger mechanism and locking devices

Designed for automatic firing only, the gun used some of the force developed by the explosion of the propellant to eject the empty cartridge, cock, reload, and fire the next round. While similar to other automatic weapons in operation, the 20mm Oerlikon did embody some important differences, among which were:
- the barrel did not recoil;
- the breechblock was never locked against the breech and was actually in motion at the moment of firing;
- there was no counterrecoil brake, the force of counterrecoil being checked by the explosion of the following round.

The 20mm fired fixed ammunition from a 60-round magazine at a cyclic rate of about 450rpm. In practice, an experienced crew could maintain a rate of about 300rpm. Usually, every other round or every third round in the spring-loaded magazine was a tracer.

TORPEDO ARMAMENT

The Sullivans carried two quintuple 21in torpedo tubes on the superstructure deck: a Mk 14 mount between the stacks and a Mk 15 mount aft of the second stack. Each mount consisted of five tubes supported by a saddle resting on the roller bearing assembly of the stand. The stand, in turn, contained a training circle. Training was normally through an electric–hydraulic drive controlled by the operation of training handwheels, although manual training was available in the event of a power failure.

TABLE 4: **PARTICULARS OF THE Mk 15 TORPEDO**

Length:	288in
Diameter:	21in
Weight:	3841lb
Propulsion:	Turbine (air-alcohol-water superheated)
Guidance:	Gyro
Warhead:	Mk 17 Mod 3
Exploder:	Mk 6 Mod 13
Range:	6000yds at 45kts
	10,000yds at 33.5kts
	15,000yds at 26.5kts

TABLE 5: **PARTICULARS OF THE Mk 44 TORPEDO**

	Mod 0	Mod 1
Length:	100in	101.3in
Diameter:	12.75in	12.75in
Weight:	425lb	433lb
Guidance:	Helix search	Helix search
Homing:	Active	Active
Warhead:	Mk 101 Mod 0	Mk 101 Mod 0
	75lb HBX-3	75lb HBX-3
Exploder:	Mk 19 Mod 12	Mk 19 Mod 12
	Contact	Contact

Each barrel assembly consisted of a main barrel, spoon, and spoon extension. The spoon and spoon extension were open on the bottom and the spoon extension was hinged at the top so that it could be folded back along the spoon to save deck space. The breech end was closed by a door to form a chamber for the powder gases which expelled the torpedo from the tube. Mounted on top of the tube assembly were a seat for the trainer and gyro setter, part of the training gear, a tube sight, the firing mechanism, and other devices.

Within the barrel, at the bottom, were rollers which facilitated loading the torpedo. Running the length of the top of the barrel to the end of the spoon extension was a T-shaped slot into which was fitted the guide stud on the torpedo. The stud prevented the torpedo from dropping downward before the tail cleared the main barrel, thus preventing damage to the tail assembly.

Impulse chambers were fitted to the aft end of the barrel. These chambers accepted the black powder charges (sodium nitrate) used to launch the torpedoes. Normally, the charges were fired electrically from the bridge, but could be fired locally by percussion.

The tubes were arranged so that speed, depth, and gyro settings could be made while the torpedoes were in the barrels. Additionally, a tripping lever was located in each barrel to trip the starting lever on the torpedo as it was launched.

The primary difference between the Mk 14 and the Mk 15 mounts was the blast shield or cupola fitted to the latter. This was a steel cylinder with a hatch on its top and a visor on its forward portion which was fitted over the trainer and gyro setter's position to protect them from the blast of mount 53. The shield was portable and was mounted with a simple rod and bracket assembly.

The Mk 15 torpedo was the standard destroyer antisurface weapon of the period. Developed in 1935 as a replacement for the smaller and less powerful Mk 11 and Mk 12 versions, the Mk 15 was a 21in diameter, turbine-driven, nearly two-ton weapon capable of delivering an 825lb warhead a maximum of 15,000yds. The Mk 15 comprised three main sections bolted together. The forward section contained 825lb of HBX and a contact exploder Mk 6, the latter mounted on the lower forward portion of the warhead. The center section contained the flask for the compressed air and the alcohol fuel. The tail section contained the turbine, gyros, and servos for the directional systems, as well as the contra-rotatingpropellers and the fins.

During her August 1945 AA refit, *The Sullivans* lost her forward Mk 14 mount, this being replaced by a pair of quad 40mm and their associated tower for the Mk 63 directors. Sometime after 1959, the aft Mk 15 mount was replaced by two triple Mk 32 ASW mounts, each mounted just aft of the waist 3in/50 positions. This may have occurred during the September 1961 overhaul. The Mk 32 mounts each carried three Mk 44 ASW torpedoes which were light-weight, electrically powered, acoustic weapons.

DEPTH CHARGES AND PROJECTORS

The Sullivans was fitted to carry the cylindrical Mk 6 and the teardrop-shaped Mk 9 charges. Two Mk 3 release tracks were fitted to the stern and three Mk 6 projectors were placed on each beam alongside the after deckhouse. Initially, a four-charge ready service rack was provided for each projector, but this was later modified to a double rack.

The Mk 6 depth charge consisted of a sheet-steel cylinder measuring 27.625in in length by 17.625in in diameter, a central tube containing a Mk 6 pistol, a booster extender, and a Mk 6 booster can containing 3.5lb of granular TNT, and 300lb of cast TNT. The pistol was adjustable and had eight indexed settings stamped on the face of the carrying flange, namely 30, 50, 100, 150, 200, 250, and 300 feet, plus 'Safe'. Sink rates varied between 6ft and 9ft per second and the effective range of relative damage was determined by BUSHIPS tests to be: 30ft fatal damage, 60ft serious damage, 90ft moderate to slight damage.

The Mk 9 depth charge was teardrop shaped and was fitted with helical fins to provide more stable underwater 'flight' characteristics. Dimensionally, the Mk 9 was similar to the Mk 6, but contained only 200lb of TNT; it did, however, have a higher sink rate (14ft per second).

The Mk 6 projector consisted of a spherical expansion chamber into which was set a 24in by 6in smooth bore tube at a 45° angle. Set perpendicular to this tube, and also at a 45° angle, was a casting which contained the breech mechanism. The breech plug was an interrupted-screw type, housing a firing mechanism which provided for local percussion firing by lanyard, or electrical firing from the bridge. The entire unit was fixed, no provisions being made for training or elevation. Variations in range were obtained by altering the weight of the impulse charge. Three standard weights of spherohexagonal black powder charges were used to obtain ranges of 50, 75, or 120 yards with a Mk 6 depth charge, and 60, 90, or 150 yards with the Mk 9 charge.

In operation, an arbor (essentially a tube with a steel tray) was fitted into the projector tube and a depth charge was chained to the arbor. Firing was accomplished by electrical or percussion ignition of an impulse charge placed in the breech, the resulting gases forcing the arbor out of the tube.

The ready service racks provided storage for four 300lb or 600lb depth charges and several arbors. The basic unit consisted of an L-shaped frame of welded angle, rollers, and a loading tray. Brackets welded to the inside rear vertical leg held a portable davit, which was used to lift the depth charges into the racks and to assist in the loading of the charges into the projector.

TABLE 6: PARTICULARS OF THE Mk 6 DEPTH CHARGE

Length:	27.625in
Diameter:	17.625in
Weights:	
Case, empty	90lb
Case, loaded, primed	390lb
Complete charge, loaded	
and primed	420lb
Charge:	300lb TNT
Exploder:	Mk 6 pistol, 3.5lb granular TNT
Sink rate:	6–9fps
Depth settings:	30ft, 50ft, 100ft, 150ft, 200ft, 250ft, 300ft
Effective radius of damage:	30ft fatal, 60ft serious, 90ft moderate to slight

HEDGEHOG

The Hedgehog (officially the 7.2in projector Mk 10) was not fitted to *The Sullivans* until after World War II, although it had been used widely by the smaller destroyer escorts with great success. As fitted to *The Sullivans*, two units, with four ready service lockers, occupied the positions filled formerly by twin 40mm mounts. Likewise, the former clipping room in the lower part of the bridge was converted to a ready service room for the 7.2in projectiles and passing scuttles were installed in its forward bulkhead.

The base frame of the projector consisted of two 18in channel beams running lengthwise and two 12in I-beams running across, forming a box. Each I-beam carried four bearings which supported the cradle assemblies, which consisted of four 10in I-beams riding on trunnion assemblies. The trunnions fitted into the bearings on the base frame and could be tilted about an axis parallel to the keel of the ship. A connecting bar tilted all four cradles simultaneously when the roll-correction gear was operated.

Six spigot sockets were welded to each cradle and held the spigots on which the charges were loaded for firing, these spigots having slightly varying vertical angles. The wires of the firing circuits passed through the spigots, the ungrounded side of which terminated in a firing pin.

The charge consisted of a cylinder 7.2in in diameter containing 30lb of TNT and the detonator, a tail section consisting of a steel tube and fins, and the impulse charge.

In operation, the projector was loaded by placing the tails of the missiles over the spigots, sliding them down, and rotating them to ensure contact between the firing pin and primer. The charges were fired by a ripple switch having twelve contacts, the missiles being fired in pairs. The interval between pair firings was about one tenth of a second and the circuits were wired so that the missiles with the highest trajectories were fired first and those with the flattest trajectories last, thus allowing the missiles to hit the water at the same time. Average range was 200yds and the spigots were so arranged that the charges fell within an elliptical pattern measuring about 140ft by 120ft. Firing to impact with the surface took about 9 seconds and the sink rate was about 4.5 seconds per 100 feet.

FIRE CONTROL EQUIPMENT

The Sullivans carried a wide variety of fire control equipment during her operational lifetime. Initially, she mounted three Mk 49 directors for her 40mm battery (two on the aft stack and one on the aft 40mm platform) and a Mk 37 Gunfire Control System (GFCS) with Mk 4 radar on her navigating bridge top. By August 1945, the Mk 49s had been replaced by lightweight Mk 51 directors with their lead-computing Mk 14 gunsights, the Mk 4 by the more effective Mk 12/22 combination, and the new Mk 63 blind-fire units had been added to the newly installed quad 40mm mounts. In her final form, *The Sullivans* retained the two amidships Mk 63s, but added a Mk 56 director aft and had a Mk 25 dish in place of the earlier Mk 12/22 combination on the Mk 37 director.

Mk 49 director: The Mk 49 was an early, and largely unsuccessful, light anti-aircraft director developed by the Ford Instrument Company. This was a power-driven, single-operator unit resembling a small turret.

Mk 51 director/Mk 14 gunsight: The Mk 51 director was a simple light-weight director consisting of a pedestal, head, and a modification of the Mk 14 gunsight. The pedestal was bolted to the deck and supported the head on ball bearings. The head supported a carriage which had a platform for mounting the gunsight. The handle bars attached to the carriage were used by the operator to move the carriage in elevation and the head in train. The right handle contained a firing key which controlled the guns when they were in director-control mode. The sight power unit, which consisted of a motor-driven air pump, was mounted on the head.

The Mk 14 gunsight, developed by Dr Charles Draper of MIT, was mounted on both the Mk 51 directors and the 20mm guns. It incorporated two gyroscopically operated mechanisms which automatically computed lead angle and superelevation. Lead angle computations were always correct for any value of trunnion tilt, and superelevation was computed and applied in the vertical plane. A luminous cross which established the sighting axis was the reflected image of an illuminated reticle. Sight movement during tracking caused the two gyscopes to precess, actuating the two mirrors which shifted the position of the cross. The offset of the cross was such that the sighting axis was displaced from the bore axis by required lead angle corrected for supereleva-tion.

Mk 63 director: The Mk 63 director was a two-unit blind-fire director intended for anti-aircraft weapons. The actual director was mounted on a pedestal similar to that of the Mk 51, while the radar antenna was mounted directly on the gun mount.

Mk 37 gunfire control system: *The Sullivans* was fitted with a single Mk 37 GFCS, the director being mounted on top of the navigating bridge. During her lifetime, she carried at least two different Mods of the director, the early unit with three hatches on the inclined face and the later unit with a large cupola to port for the mount control officer. This cupola, or cockpit, was fitted with a slewing sight and usually fitted with a canvas dodger for weather protection. The Mk 37 GFCS consisted of three main components:

- a Mk 37 director
- a Mk 6 stable element
- a Mk 1 computer

The *Mk 37 director* consisted of a weld-steel shield enclosing three director telescopes and a Mk 42 stereoscopic range finder mounted on a carriage which was supported by roller bearings on a base ring. The base ring rested on a director foundation, through which the crew of six or seven men entered the shield. The *Mk 6 stable element* was a complex instrument designed to:

- stabilize director optics
- compute target elevation from director elevation
- compute relative target bearing from director train
- compute gun trunnion-tilt corrections
- compute searchlight trunnion-tilt corrections

- control the firing instant in selected level or selected cross-level fire, either by automatically closing the firing circuit or by indicating visually that the circuit should be closed

Mounted in the plotting room, the Mk 6 had an associated control and follow-up panel, and a motor generator.

The *Mk 1 computer* was mounted next to the Mk 6 stable element in the plotting room. This computer was designed to make all of the required calculations that can be computed centrally for the 5in/38 battery. Its essential functions were to:

- aid the director personnel in keeping director line of sight on the target
- permit the 5in/38 guns to be pointed and trained, and fuzes and sights to be set continuously for AA or surface fire against a common target, and
- permit the main battery to be pointed and trained, and the sights to be set for AA fire at a common target, using a selected value of fuze setting

Fire control radar: *The Sullivans* mounted a variety of fire control radar antennae during and post-World War II. In order of use, these antennae were:

- Mk 4 – mounted on a stabilized framework on top of the Mk 37 director, this radar consisted of a 6ft × 6ft antenna with a right-up, left-down lobing pattern
- Mk 12 – similar in shape and size to the Mk 4, this unit used a shorter wavelength and incorporated improvements such as automatic range tracking and range rate measurement
- Mk 22 – a parabolic height-finder, this unit was designed to operate in conjunction with either the Mk 4 or the Mk 12
- Mk 25 – lightweight, dish antenna which replaced the Mk 12/22 combina-tion post-World War II

Mk 27 torpedo director: Initially, *The Sullivans* carried two Mk 27 directors in the bridge wings. By 1959, only one was fitted, this on a platform attached to the aft stack.

The torpedo director system on *The Sullivans* included three major compo-nents: a Mk 27 director, a torpedo-course indicator on the tubes, and the associated transmission and communication systems. The Mk 27 director consisted of a stand, case, and telescope unit. The stand was bolted to the deck and supported the case on ball bearings. A training circle secured to the stand meshed with a gear driven by a training wheel mounted in the case and provided about 390° of train. The case housed the units used to solve the torpedo problem, transmit the basic torpedo course and gyro angle to the tubes, and receive own-ship course from the gyro computer. The telescope unit consisted of a tiltable mirror and fixed-prism telescope mounted on a pivot. The tiltable mirror made it possible to hold the LOS on the target in

TABLE 7: PARTICULARS OF SHIP'S BOAT

Type:	26ft motor whaleboat Mk 1
Length overall:	26ft ⅜in
Beam:	7ft 4⅝in
Draft:	2ft 4in loaded
Displacement:	8850lb
Construction:	Round bottom, wood frame, carvel planked
Power plant:	One 4-cylinder Navy type DA 25hp diesel
Propeller:	One 18in diameter by 25in pitch, right-hand rotation
Speed:	7kts loaded
Fuel capacity:	28 gallons
Range:	110 nautical miles at full power and full load

elevation as the ship pitched and rolled. The torpedo course indicator was mounted directly on the tubes and received the outputs generated by the Mk 27 director. These outputs were used to set torpedo gyro angle and tube train mechanically.

CAMOUFLAGE

Photographic evidence suggests that *The Sullivans* carried at least three different camouflage Measures between her February 1943 commissioning and final decommissioning in January 1965. Between 1943 and her AA refit in August 1945, *The Sullivans* was painted in Measure 11 (overall Sea Blue, 5-S). During the AA refit, this scheme was replaced with Measure 22 (Navy Blue, 5-N and Haze Gray, 5-H). At some point post-World War II, perhaps during her 1952 refit for Korean War duty, *The Sullivans* received a coat of Measure 17 Ocean Gray (5–O). Quite possibly, at some time between 1952 and 1976, she may also have been painted in Measure 27 (overall Haze Gray, 5-H); however, no photographic evidence indicating this was available to the author.

Throughout most of her service life, *The Sullivans* carried a large green shamrock outlined in white on both sides of her forward funnel and a smaller version on either bow of her two 26ft motor whaleboats. During one of her post-war refits, the design was changed, the white outline giving way to a white disc. The shamrock also seems to have been altered somewhat, the petals becoming rounder and fuller than the original design.

The Photographs

2, 3 Two aerial views of *The Sullivans* show her initial configuration to good effect. Note the triangular shape of the aft 20mm shield and the prominent Mk 49 directors on the aft 40mm platform and aft stack.

USN via A D Baker III

4. *The Sullivans* in San Francisco Bay, 12 October 1943. At this time, she is carrying Measure 11 (overall Sea Blue 5-S). The cylindrical objects on the aft stack and the director tower aft are Mk 49 directors, which were eventually replaced by the more effective Mk 51. Antennae for SC-2, SG, and TBS are visible on the foremast, while the Mk 37 director mounts a Mk 4 radar

USN via A D Baker III

5. Taken by a passing aircraft in October 1943, this photo shows the classic *Fletcher* class profile.

USN via A D Baker III

6. *The Sullivans* at Mare Island, 30 August 1945, alongside a *Benson* class DD. This view shows *The Sullivans* following her 1945 AA refit. Of note in this photo are the ECM 'sword' antenna just below the range light and the late Mod Mk 37 director. Originally, she had been fitted with the earlier Mod which did not have the large mount captain's cupola to port.

USN via A D Baker III

7. Taken on 30 August 1945 at Mare Island, this photo shows some of the modifications made to *The Sullivans* during her AA refit. Among the items identified with a white half circle are:

- a UHF antenna on the foremast
- 'ski pole' IFF antenna on the yardarm
- Mk 51 directors in place of the earlier Mk 14 torpedo tubes
- ECM antenna on the aft stack
- two twin 20mm Mk 24 mounts in the waist
- ECM antennae on a pole mast mounted on the aft
  Mk 51 director tower

USN via A D Baker III

NOT TO BE RELEAS
FOR PUBLICATION
NAVY YARD MARE ISLAND, C

RESTRICTED

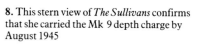

8. This stern view of *The Sullivans* confirms that she carried the Mk 9 depth charge by August 1945

USN via A D Baker III

9, 10. These two shots show off the aft 3in/50 platform and its associated Mk 56 director and tower. The rectangular frames along the deck edge held inflatable liferafts, which superseded the floater nets of World War II. The heavy tubular frame just below the gunshield is the aft refueling-at-sea station, the standpipe for which is just below the large, white-painted cleat on the bulkhead.

(Caption on previous page)

11. Initially, *The Sullivans* mounted single Mk 4 20mm in the waist. By 1945, these had been replaced with twin Mk 24 mounts. The forward mount in this photo shows the pump for the air compressor which powered the Mk 14 gunsight mounted on the crossbar of the shield. The handlebars with their associated trigger are seen to good advantage just below the shoulder pad.

P Ross

12. An interesting view of the quintuple torpedo tubes. The T-shaped slot visible in the end of the spoon extension is for a guide lug on the torpedo.

P Ross

13. Aft torpedo handling crane in lowered position, showing mount for refueling-at-sea gear on top of the pedestal. This particular shot was taken aboard *Kidd* in 1986, but is identical to the unit carried by *The Sullivans*.

P Ross

14. Following her post-World War II refits, *The Sullivans* had her remaining 21in torpedo tube replaced with two Mk 32 launchers. These units were mounted just aft of the waist 3in/50 positions and appear to have been mounted after 1959, as the plans for the 1959 refit do not show them.

K Kalb

15. Starboard Mk 10 Hedgehog launcher and ready service locker for the 7.2in projectiles onboard *The Sullivans*, 1987. The circular, hinged cover to the right rear of the launcher is a passing scuttle for the projectiles.

K Kalb

16. 7.2in projectile ready service locker, showing 'honeycomb' interior for projectile storage.

K Kalb

17. *The Sullivans'* pole foremast was replaced by this large tripod mast after World War II to meet the demands of an increasing need for radar and ECM antennae. Visible in this photo are the AN/SPS-10 (top), AN/SPS-6C (large antenna), several whip antennae, and the Mk 25 dish for fire control.

K Kalb

18. Back of the bridge showing tripod mast and forward stack details.

P Ross

19. Detail view of the 12in signal lamp on the bridge wing.

P Ross

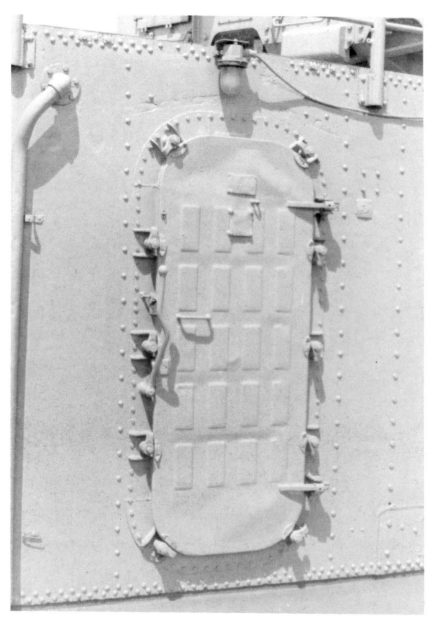

20. Typical superstructure watertight door.

P Ross

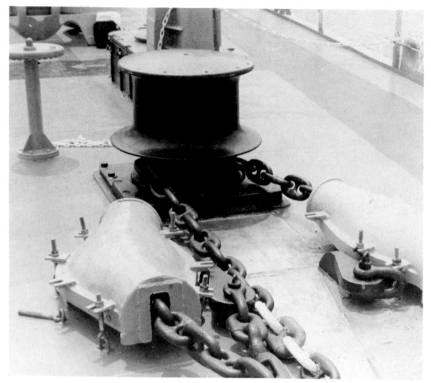

21. Close-up of the capstan, chainpipe covers, and capstan brake.

K Kalb

22. *The Sullivans* carried two 26ft motor
whaleboats Mk 1 throughout World War II.
This particular boat is an earlier version with a
light sheet metal canopy and a more
rectangular engine cover, but is essentially the
same as *The Sullivans'* boats.

USN via Tom Walkowiak

23. Details of the boat davits are shown to good advantage in this starboard view of *Kidd*. The boat is a post-World War II 26ft motor whaleboat Mk II made of fiberglass.

P Ross

The Drawings

In order to make the best use of the page size the drawings have been reproduced to the scale of 1/256 (3/64 of an inch = 1 foot), with large scale drawings usually in multiples of that – 1/128, 1/64 and 1/32 (respectively 3/32, 3/16 and 3/8 of an inch = 1 foot).

A General arrangements

A1 **OUTBOARD PROFILE (October 1943; all drawings in this section, except A31–33, are 1/256 scale)**

A1

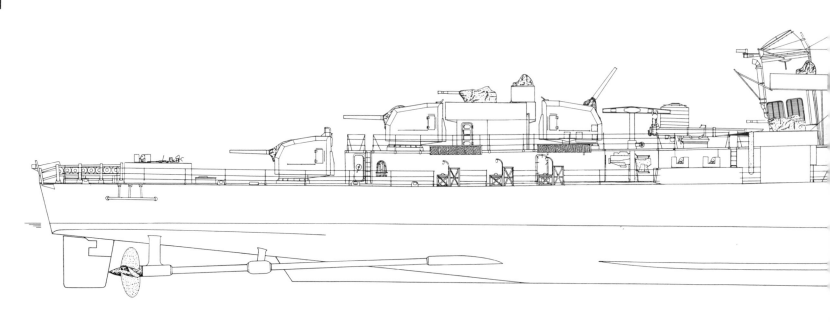

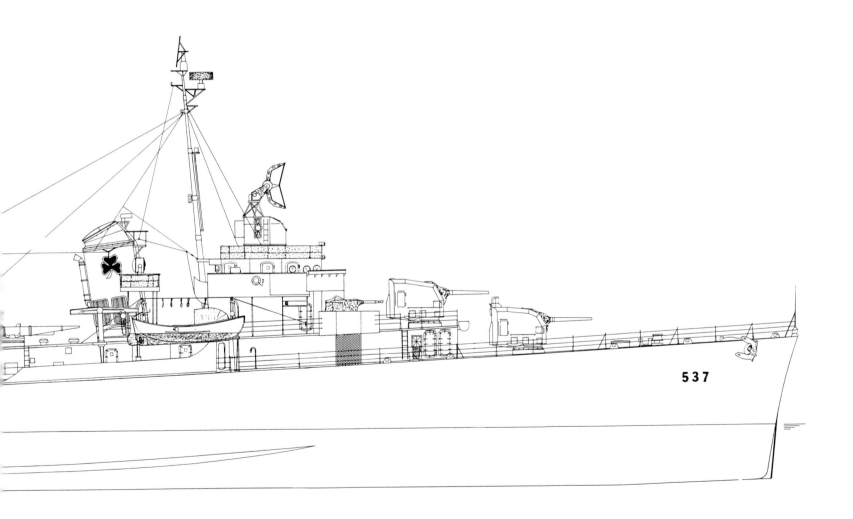

537

A General arrangements

A2

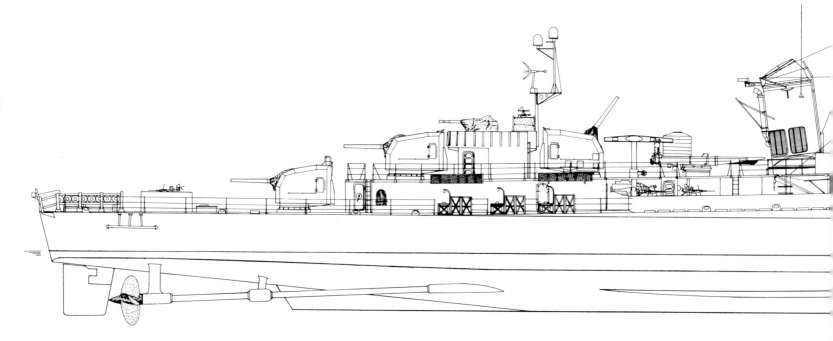

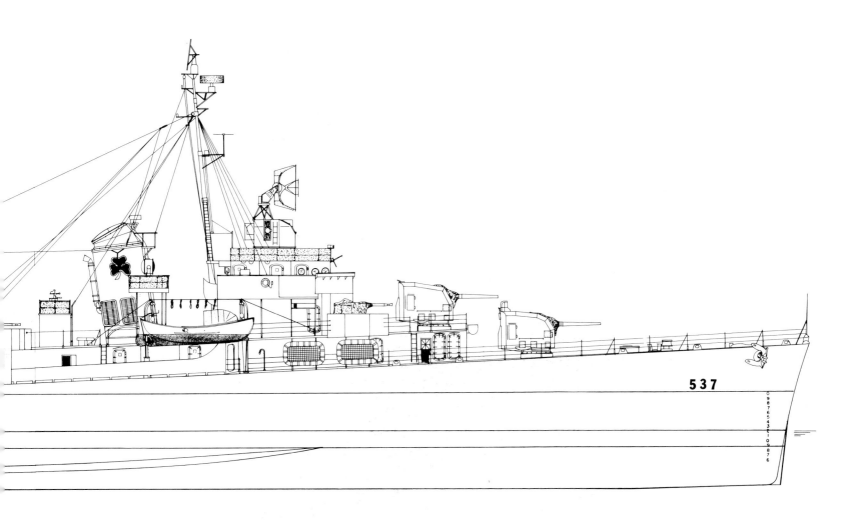

537

A General arrangements

A3

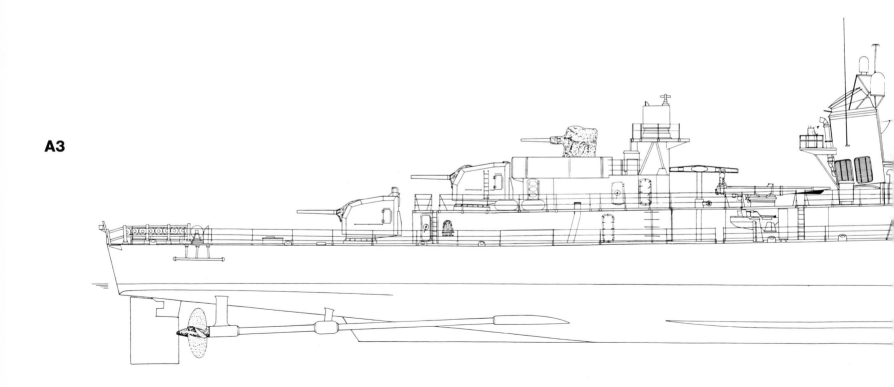

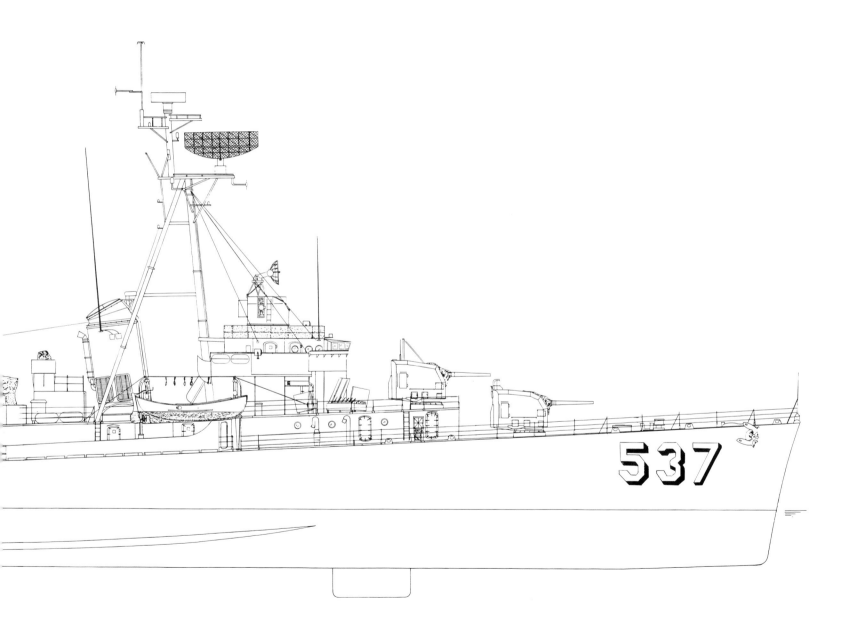

537

A General arrangements

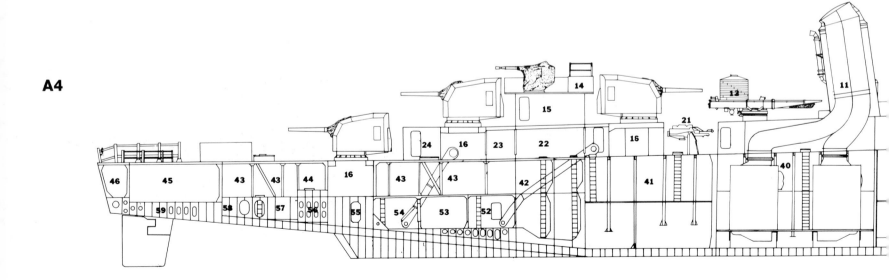

A4

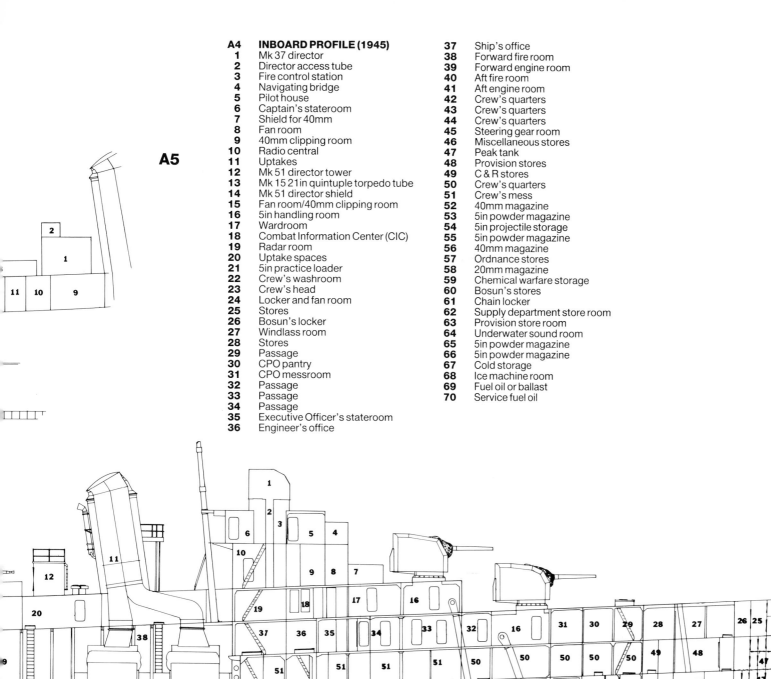

A4   INBOARD PROFILE (1945)

1 Mk 37 director
2 Director access tube
3 Fire control station
4 Navigating bridge
5 Pilot house
6 Captain's stateroom
7 Shield for 40mm
8 Fan room
9 40mm clipping room
10 Radio central
11 Uptakes
12 Mk 51 director tower
13 Mk 15 21in quintuple torpedo tube
14 Mk 51 director shield
15 Fan room/40mm clipping room
16 5in handling room
17 Wardroom
18 Combat Information Center (CIC)
19 Radar room
20 Uptake spaces
21 5in practice loader
22 Crew's washroom
23 Crew's head
24 Locker and fan room
25 Stores
26 Bosun's locker
27 Windlass room
28 Stores
29 Passage
30 CPO pantry
31 CPO messroom
32 Passage
33 Passage
34 Passage
35 Executive Officer's stateroom
36 Engineer's office
37 Ship's office
38 Forward fire room
39 Forward engine room
40 Aft fire room
41 Aft engine room
42 Crew's quarters
43 Crew's quarters
44 Crew's quarters
45 Steering gear room
46 Miscellaneous stores
47 Peak tank
48 Provision stores
49 C & R stores
50 Crew's quarters
51 Crew's mess
52 40mm magazine
53 5in powder magazine
54 5in projectile storage
55 5in powder magazine
56 40mm magazine
57 Ordnance stores
58 20mm magazine
59 Chemical warfare storage
60 Bosun's stores
61 Chain locker
62 Supply department store room
63 Provision store room
64 Underwater sound room
65 5in powder magazine
66 5in powder magazine
67 Cold storage
68 Ice machine room
69 Fuel oil or ballast
70 Service fuel oil

A5

A General arrangements

A6 MAIN DECK LEVEL (1945)
1 Fan room/Landing force equipment
2 5in handling room
3 Fan room/repair party equipment
4 Wardroom
5 Wardroom pantry
6 Passage
7 Combat Information Center
8 Division Commander's stateroom
9 Radar operating room
10 Head
11 Landing force equipment
12 Vegetable locker
13 Uptake space
14 Vent fan and deck gear
15 Vegetable preparation space
16 Galley
17 Laundry
18 Provision issue room
19 Battery charging room
20 Mk 63 radar and power drive control room
21 Post office
22 Emergency radio room
23 Mail room
24 20mm ready service room
25 Crew's washroom
26 Crew's head
27 Repair locker and fan space

A7 SUPERSTRUCTURE DECK LEVEL (1945)
1 Fan room
2 Coding room
3 Radio central
4 40mm ready service room
5 Navigation and chart room
6 Passage
7 Mk 51 director tower
8 Stack
9 Machine gun radar room
10 40mm ready service room
11 Fan room and gun crew shelter

A8 BRIDGE
1 Pilot house
2 Fire control station
3 Sea cabin washroom
4 Head
5 Sonar room
6 Passage

A9 Mk 51 DIRECTOR TOWER

A10 40mm PLATFORM (1945)

A11 TOP OF NAVIGATING BRIDGE (1945)

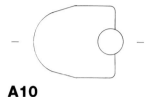

A10

A7

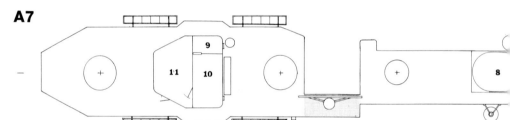

A6

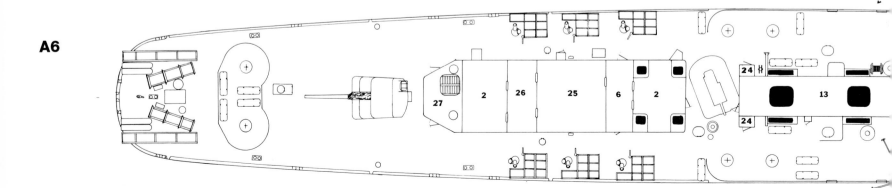

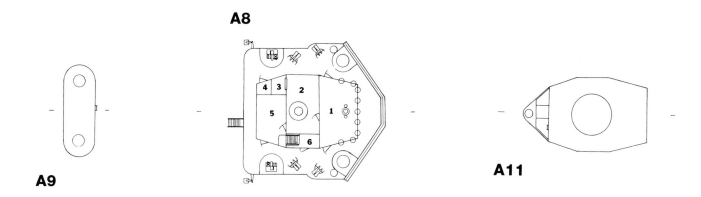

A8

A9

A11

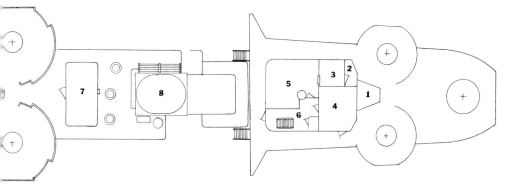

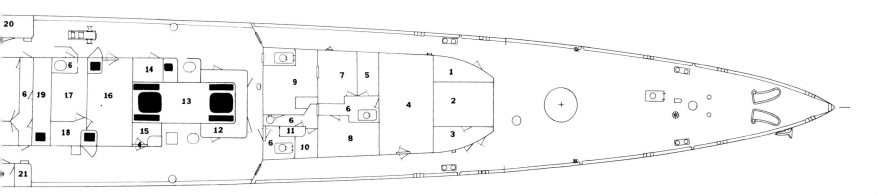

A General arrangements

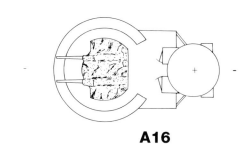

A16

A13

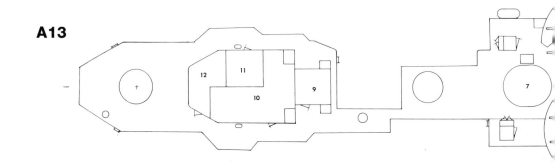

A12

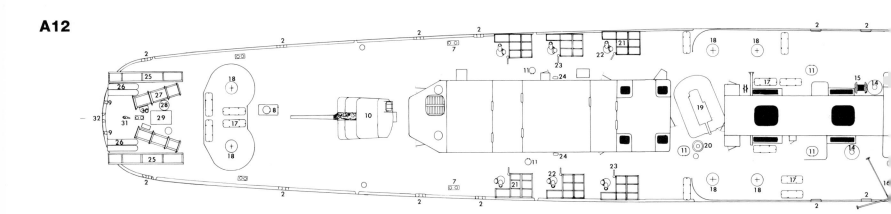

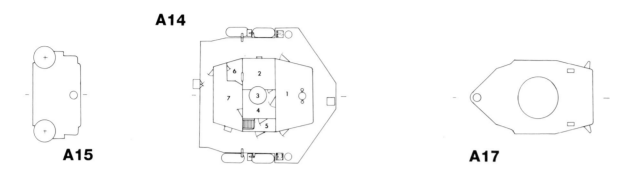

A14

A15　　　　　　　　　　　　　**A17**

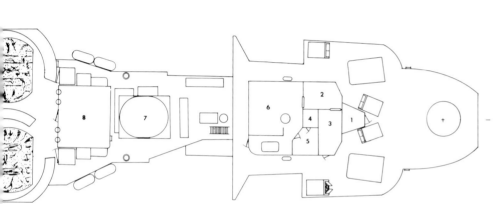

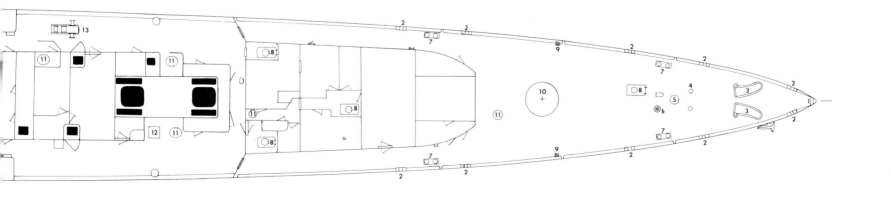

A General arrangements

A18

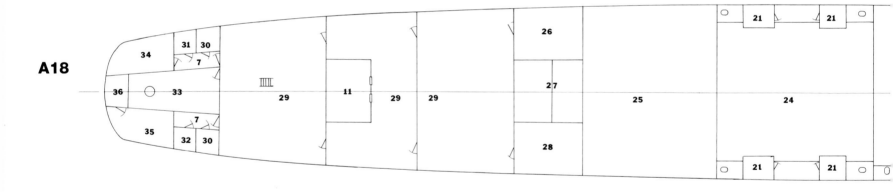

A19

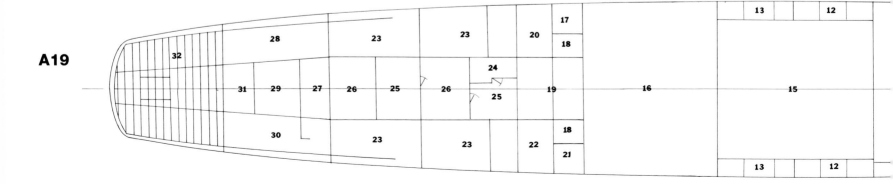

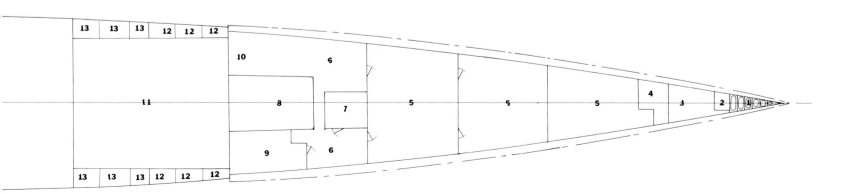

A19 SECOND PLATFORM DECK (1945)

1	Peak tank
2	AT trunk
3	Provision storeroom
4	C & R stores
5	Crew's quarters
6	Crew's mess
7	Scullery
8	Fuel oil service tank
9	Diesel generator room
10	Bread locker
11	Forward fire room
12	Freshwater tanks
13	Reserve feed water tanks
14	Forward engine room
15	Aft fire room
16	Aft engine room
17	Fuel oil service tank
18	Stuffing box compartment
19	Fuel oil service tank
20	Diesel oil
21	Fuel oil separating tank
22	Fuel oil or ballast
23	Fuel oil or ballast
24	20mm magazine
25	5in handling room
26	5in powder magazine
27	40mm magazine
28	Engineering stores
29	Ordnance stores
30	Bulk stores
31	20mm magazine
32	Chemical warfare material

55

A General arrangements

A21

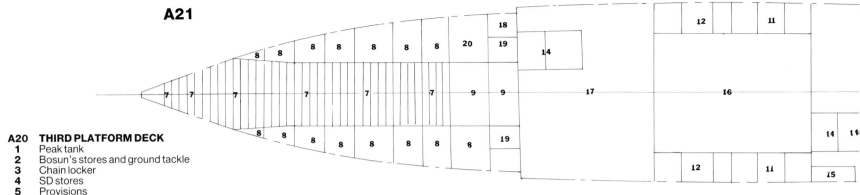

A20 THIRD PLATFORM DECK
1 Peak tank
2 Bosun's stores and ground tackle
3 Chain locker
4 SD stores
5 Provisions
6 Underwater sound room
7 5in powder magazine
8 5in handling room
9 Meat room
10 Cold storage
11 Fruits and vegetables
12 Butter and eggs
13 Ice machine room

A21 HOLD (1945)
1 Peak tank
2 Paints and inflammable liquids
3 Supply department stores
4 Rod meter compartment/Sea chest
5 Small arms
6 40mm magazine
7 Void
8 Fuel oil or ballast
9 Fuel oil service tank
10 Forward fire room
11 Freshwater tanks
12 Reserve feed water tanks
13 Forward engine room
14 Lube oil tanks
15 Lube oil settling tank
16 Aft fire room
17 Aft engine room
18 Fuel oil separating tank
19 Stuffing box compartment
20 Diesel oil

A22 FRAME 5 (looking forward)
1 Bosun's stores
2 Peak tank

A23 FRAME 22 (looking forward)
1 CPO messroom
2 Crew's quarters
3 Underwater soundroom
4 Rodmeter compartment

A24 FRAME 48 (looking forward)
1 Vent fan and heater room
2 5in handling room
3 Vent fan and 40mm control
4 Officer's stateroom
5 Passage
6 Crew's mess
7 Butter and eggs locker
8 Vegetable locker
9 Meat room

A25 FRAME 68 (looking forward)
1 Mk 37 director control tower
2 Trunk
3 Light lock
4 Firecontrol station
5 Firecontrol station
6 Passage
7 Radio central
8 Passage
9 Landing force equipment
10 Passage
11 Bread locker
12 Radar operating room
13 Ship's office
14 Passage
15 IC and plotting room
16 Crew's quarters
17 Diesel generator room
18 Fuel oil service tank
19 Food service and crew's mess
20 Fuel oil or ballast

A26 MIDSHIP SECTION (looking forward)
1 Mk 51 director tower
2 Supply office
3 Medical storeroom
4 Emergency radio room
5 Engine room

A27 FRAME 150 (looking aft)
1 Machine gun radar room
2 40mm ready service room
3 Crew's washroom
4 General workshop and electrical shop
5 Crew's quarters
6 Engineer's stores
7 Stuffing box compartment
8 Fuel oil service tank
9 Fuel oil separating tank

A22

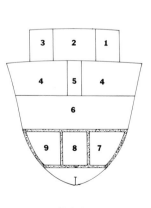

A23

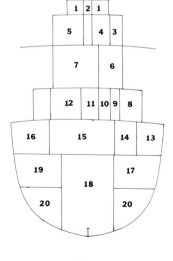

A24

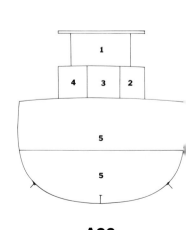

A25

A26

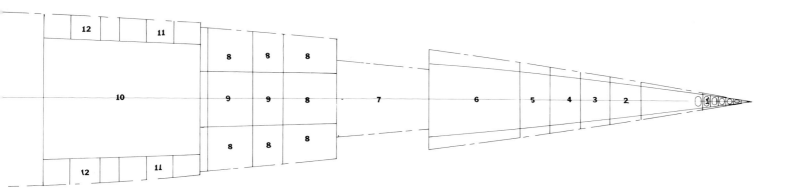

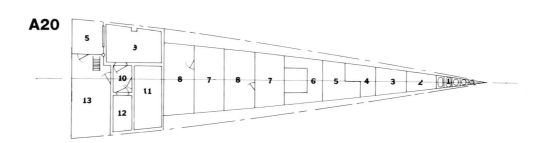

A28 FRAME 168 (looking aft)
1 Locker and fan space
2 Crew's quarters
3 Fuel oil or ballast
4 5in powder magazine
5 Fuel oil or ballast

A29 FRAME 184 (looking aft)
1 Crew's quarters
2 Engineering stores
3 40mm magazine
4 Bulk stores

A30 FRAME 206 (looking aft)
1 20mm magazine
2 Steering gear room
3 Carpenter and shipfitter shop
4 Chemical warfare stores

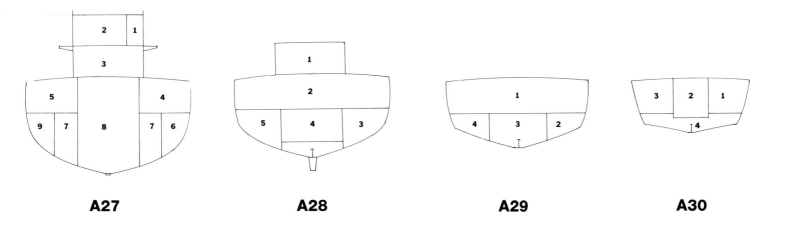

A27   **A28**   **A29**   **A30**

A General arrangements

A31

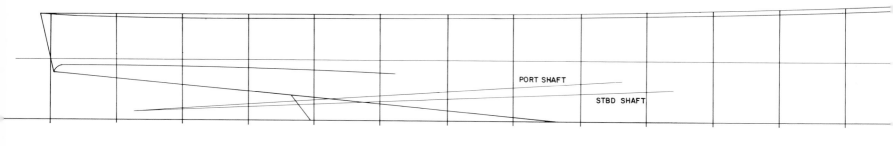

PORT SHAFT

STBD SHAFT

A32

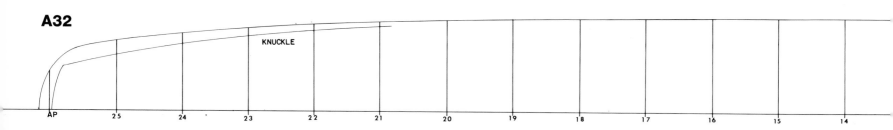

KNUCKLE

AP   25   24   23   22   21   20   19   18   17   16   15   14

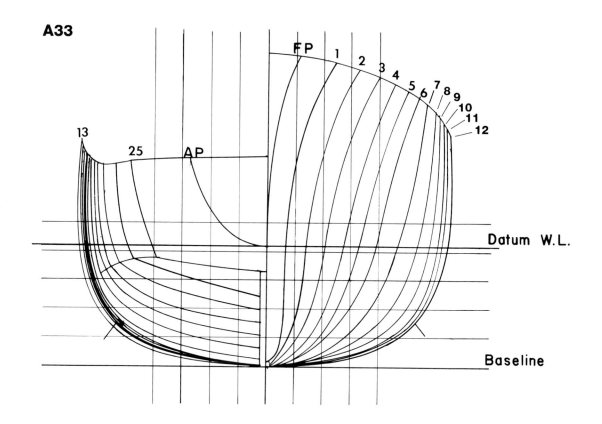

A33

FP 1 2 3 4 5 6 7 8 9 10 11 12

13 25 AP

Datum W.L.

Baseline

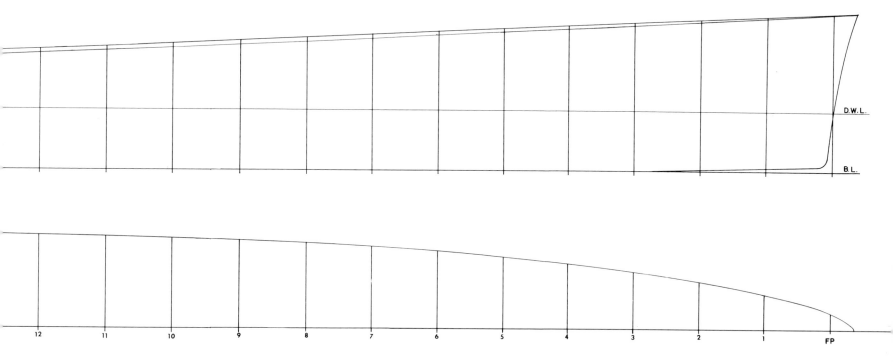

D.W.L.

B.L.

12 11 10 9 8 7 6 5 4 3 2 1 FP

B Hull construction

B1   **FRAME 12 (All drawings in this section are 1/85 scale)**

B2   **FRAME 32**

B3   **FRAME 152 (showing representative plate types and thicknesses)**
1   15# HTS
2   20# STS
3   25# STS
4   17.5# HTS
5   12# HTS
6   20# HTS

B4   **FRAME 178**

B5   **FRAME 205 (showing rudder post and rudder)**

B1

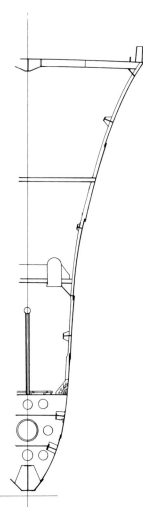

B2

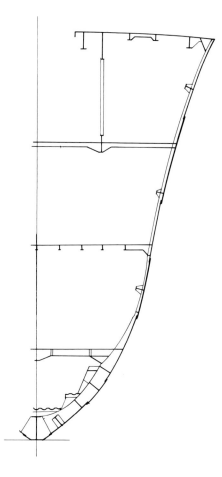

B3

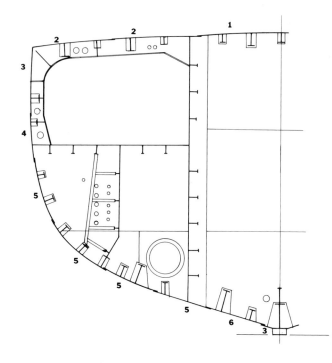

B4

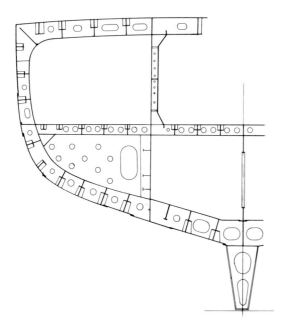

B5

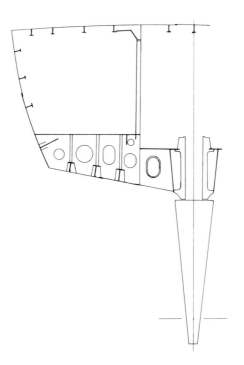

C Machinery

C1 **AFT FIRE ROOM AND ENGINE ROOM (plan view at second platform level; 1/256 scale)**

C2 **AFT FIRE ROOM AND ENGINE ROOM (inboard profile; 1/256 scale)**

1 Boiler
2 Forced draft blower
3 Uptakes
4 Low-pressure turbine
5 Gauge board
6 Main condenser
7 Main reduction gear
8 Lighting transformers
9 Turbo-generator
10 Main air ejector
11 Main circulating pump
12 Main feed pumps
13 Main switchboard
14 Auxiliary condenser air ejector
15 Deaerating feed tank

C1

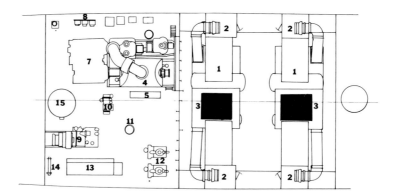

C2

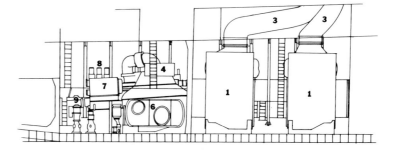

C3   MAIN FEED BOOSTER PUMP

C3/1   Side view

C3/2   Front view

C3/3   Top view
   1   Motor
   2   Air inlet
   3   Air outlet
   4   Mounting flange
   5   Pump body
   6   Suction
   7   Impeller casing
   8   Discharge
   9   Shaft bearing casing

C3/1

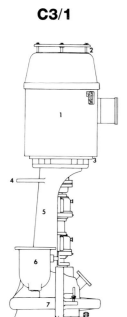

C3/2

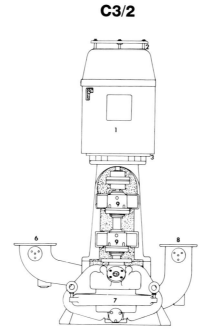

C3/3

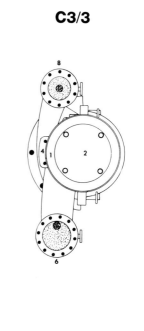

C Machinery

C4/1

C4/2

C4/3

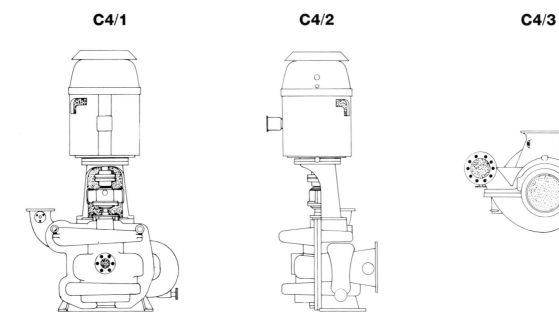

C5/1

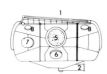

C5/3

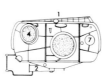

C5/2

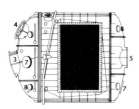

C5/4

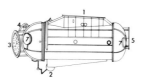

C6

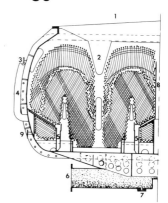

C Machinery

C7   LONGITUDINAL SECTION THROUGH PORT MAIN CONDENSER (1/40 scale)

1   40in circulating water inlet
2   29.75in auxiliary circulating water inlet
3   1¼in hose gate valve connection
4   Zinc protector plate access cover
5   Inlet water chest
6   2in water relief valve connection
7   Handhole cover
8   1in vent connection
9   0.75in test connection
10   Expansion joint
11   6in air outlet
12   Tube plate
13   10in condensate outlet
14   Support plates
15   Air baffle plates
16   Tubes
17   Gage glass connection
18   Sway bracing lug
19   Sway bracing lug
20   1in drain connection
21   Zinc protector plate access cover
22   Handhold cover
23   0.75in vent connection
24   30in circulating water inlet

C8   WATER RELIEF VALVE FOR MAIN CONDENSERS

1   Cap
2   Lever
3   Adjusting screw
4   Spring
5   Stem
6   Valve body

C9   AUXILIARY AIR EJECTOR

C10   LEFT-HAND AUXILIARY CONDENSER (1/128 scale)

C10/1 End view

C10/2 Side view

1   14in steam inlet
2   2½in condensate outlet
3   5in auxiliary steam inlet
4   7in circulating water inlet
5   6in circulating water outlet
6   Handhole cover
7   Zinc protector plate access cover
8   2in inlet from fresh water drain tank vent
9   0.75in make-up connection
10   1in recirculating connection
11   1in inlet from intercooler drain
12   3in air outlet

C9

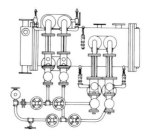

C8

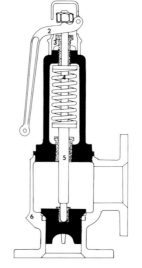

C7

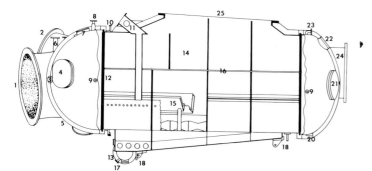

C10/1   C10/2

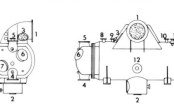

C11 RIGHT-HAND AUXILIARY CONDENSER

C11/1 Longitudinal section

C11/2 Transverse section
1 14in steam inlet
2 2½in condensate outlet
3 5in auxiliary steam inlet
4 7in circulating water inlet
5 6in circulating water outlet
6 3in air outlet
7 1in inlet from intercooler drain
8 1in recirculating connection
9 1in relief valve connection
10 Handhole cover
11 Zinc protector plate access cover
12 1in drain connection
13 Tube plate
14 Support plates
15 0.75in boiling-out connection

C12 MAIN AIR EJECTOR SERVING PORT MAIN CONDENSER

C12/1 End view

C12/2 Side view
1 ½in relief valve
2 5in tube nest inlet
3 5in tube nest outlet
4 5½in first stage air inlet
5 ½in first stage steam inlet
6 4½in atmospheric exhaust
7 Primary diffuser
8 4in gland seal section exhaust port

C12/1   C12/2

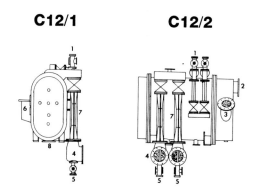

C11/1

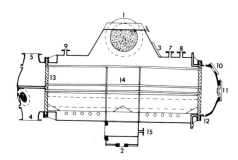

C11/2

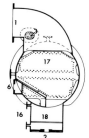

C13 FEEDWATER REGULATOR VALVE

C13/1 End view

C13/2 Longitudinal cross-section

C13/1   C13/2

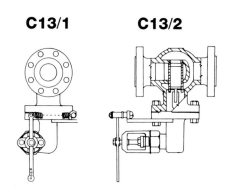

D Accommodation

Note: Symbol key applies to all drawings in this section, which are 1/256 scale

D1 **FORWARD SUPERSTRUCTURE**
1 Wardroom sofa
2 Mess table
3 Shower in Division Commander's stateroom

D2 **AFT SUPERSTRUCTURE**
1 Shower in crew's washroom

D3 **FIRST PLATFORM DECK (forward)**
1 Shelves
2 Large mess table
3 Mess table
4 Counter with sink in CPO galley
5 Desk
6 Shower

D4 **FIRST PLATFORM DECK (aft)**
1 Shower

D5 **SECOND PLATFORM DECK**
1 Mess tables
2 Steam table
3 Steam kettle
4 Ice cream freezer and cabinet

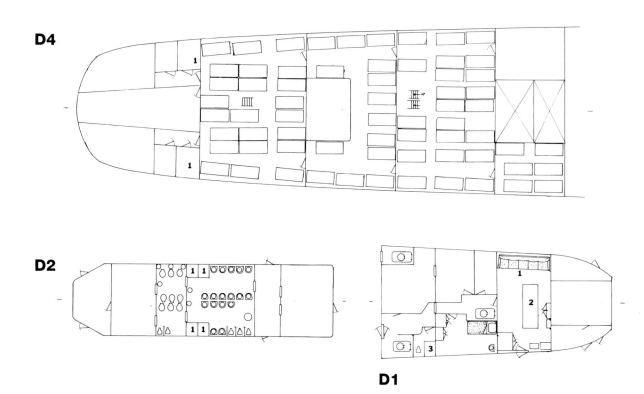

D4

D2

D1

D3

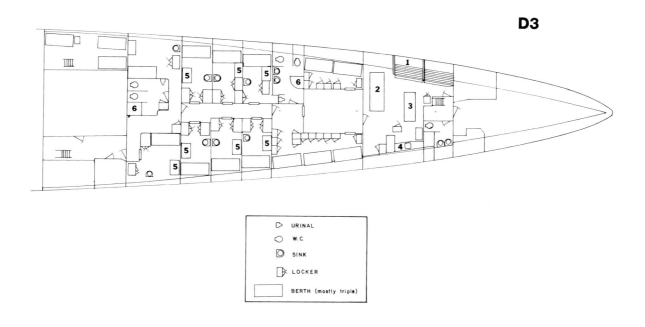

▷	URINAL
◊	W.C.
◎	SINK
⬓	LOCKER
▭	BERTH (mostly triple)

D5

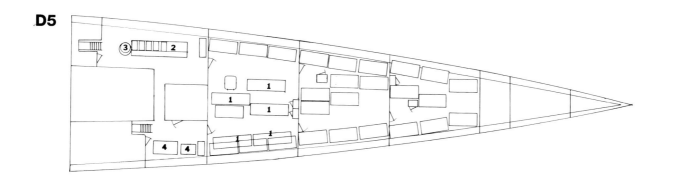

E Superstructure

E1 FORWARD SUPERSTRUCTURE
(1943; all drawings in this section
are 1/256 scale)

1 Mk 4 radar
2 Mk 37 director
3 Rangelight
4 Loudspeaker
5 Mk 27 torpedo director
6 12in signal light
7 Flag bag
8 Sidelight
9 Twin 40mm Mk 1
10 36in searchlight
11 Torpedo crane
12 21in torpedo tube Mk 14
13 Standard compass
14 Vent

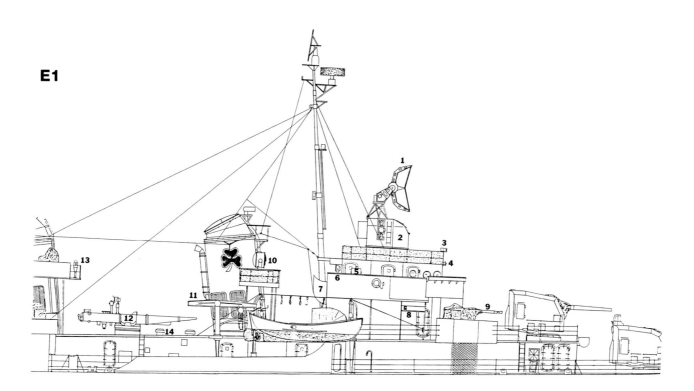

E1

E2　FORWARD SUPERSTRUCTURE (1945)

1　Mk 12/22 radar
2　Mk 37 director
3　Rangelight
4　ECM antenna
5　Mk 27 torpedo director
6　12in signal light
7　Flag bag
8　Sidelight
9　Twin 40mm Mk 1
10　36in searchlight
11　Mk 51 director
12　Quad 40mm Mk 2 with Mk 63 firecontrol radar

E2

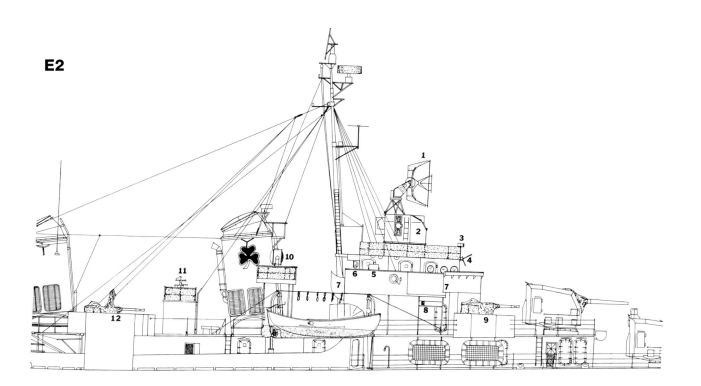

E3 **FORWARD SUPERSTRUCTURE**
(1959)
1 Mk 25 radar
2 Mk 37 director
3 12in searchlight, port and starboard
4 Rangelight
5 Bridge windshield
6 12in signal light
7 Inflatable life rafts
8 Ready service locker for 7.2in
 projectiles
9 ASW projector Mk 10
10 Mk 63 director
11 Twin 3in/50 Mk 27

E3

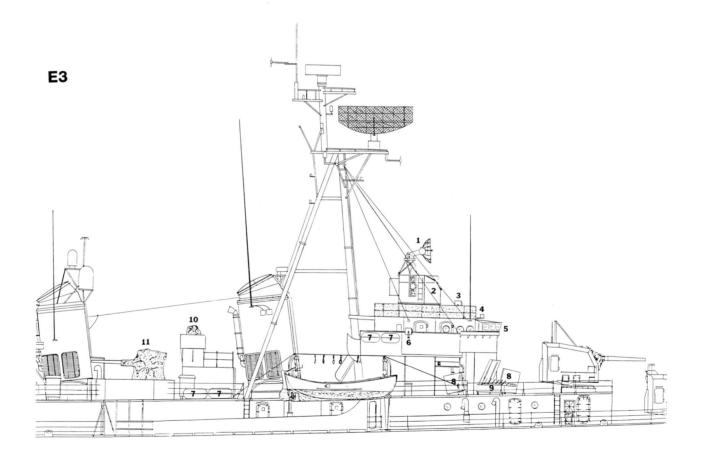

E4 AFT SUPERSTRUCTURE (1943)
1 Mk 49 director
2 Twin 40mm Mk 1
3 Quintuple 21in torpedo tube Mk 15
4 Torpedo crane
5 5in/38 Mk 30
6 Floater nets

E4

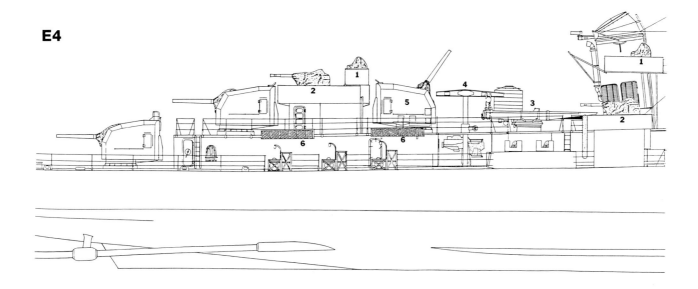

E5 **AFT SUPERSTRUCTURE (1945)**
1 Quintuple 21in torpedo tube Mk 15
2 Torpedo crane
3 5in/38 Mk 30
4 Mk 51 director
5 Twin 40mm Mk 1
6 Floater nets

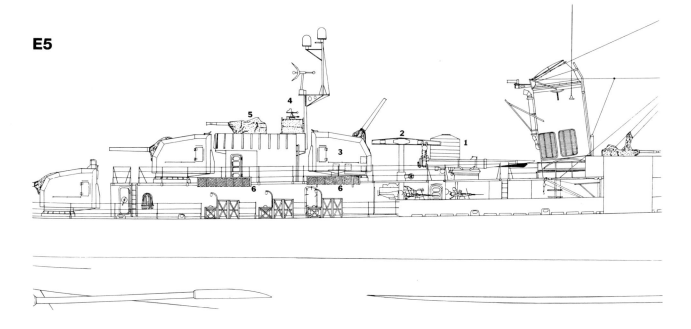

E5

E6   AFT SUPERSTRUCTURE (1959)
1   Quintuple 21in torpedo tube Mk 14
2   Torpedo crane
3   Mk 56 director
4   3in/50 ready service locker
5   Gun gear locker
6   Twin 3in/50 Mk 27
7   Inflatable life rafts
8   Torpedo director Mk 27
9   Fuel oil fill
10 Vertical reel

E6

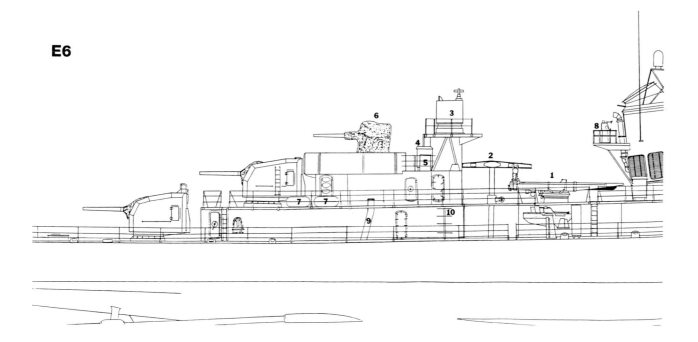

E Superstructure

E7   SUPERSTRUCTURE DECK LEVEL (1945)
1   5in/38 Mk 30
2   Twin 40mm Mk 1
3   Damage control shores storage
4   Escape scuttle
5   Vents
6   Airplane crash kit
7   Quad 40mm Mk 2
8   Standard compass
9   Vertical triple reel
10   Mk 15 torpedo tube mount
11   Torpedo crane
12   Floater nets
13   Spare 40mm barrels

E8   NAVIGATING BRIDGE (1945)

E8/1   Deck level

E8/2   Top of bridge
1   Mk 51 director mount
2   Compass
3   Pelorus
4   Skywatch station
5   Mk 27 torpedo director
6   12in signal light

E9   Mk 51 DIRECTOR TOWER

E10   40mm PLATFORM (1945)
1   Mk 51 director
2   Twin 40mm Mk 2

E11   40mm PLATFORM (1943)
1   Mk 49 director
2   Passing scuttles
3   Twin 40mm Mk 2

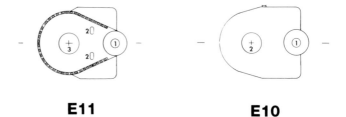

E11   **E10**

E7

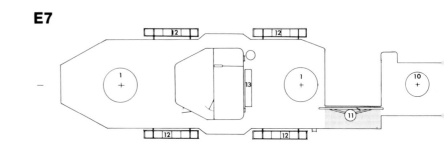

E8/1

E8/2

E9

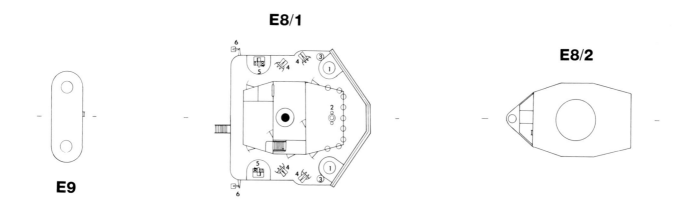

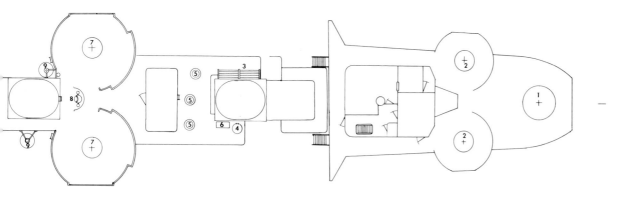

E Superstructure

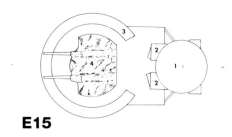

E15

E12

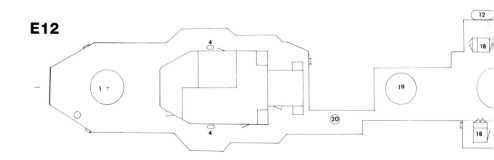

E14

E13

E16

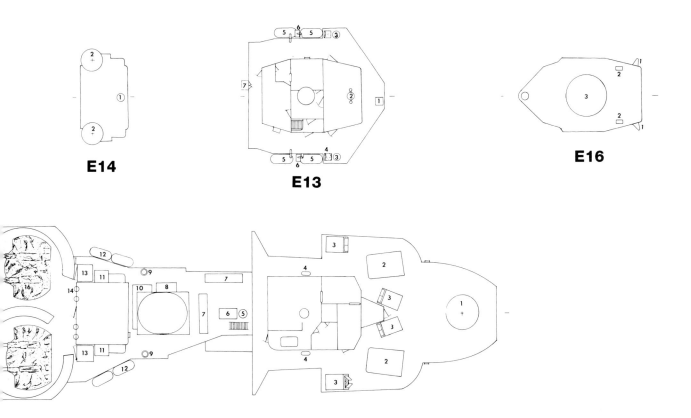

F1 **RIG (1943; all drawings in this section are 1/256 scale)**
  1 SC-2 radar
  2 SG radar
  3 Transmitting antenna
  4 TBL transmitting antenna
  5 Backstay bridle
  6 TAJ transmitting antenna
  7 Forestay
  8 Receiving antenna
  9 Mk 4 radar antenna
  10 Transmitting antenna
  11 TBL antenna lead-in
  12 TBK antenna lead-in

F1

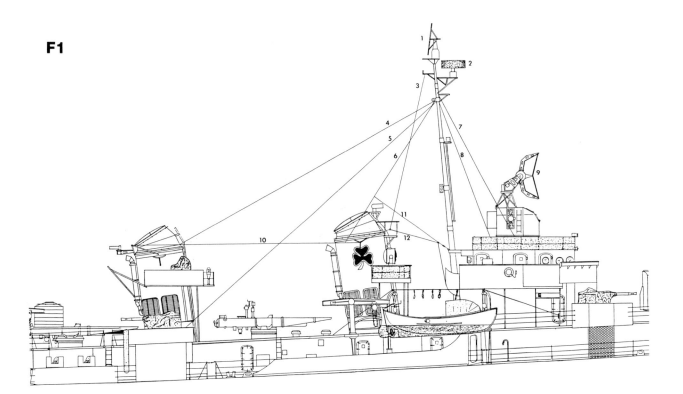

F2   **RIG (1945)**
1   SC-4 radar
2   SG radar
3   Transmitting antenna
4   TBL transmitting antenna
5   Transmitting antenna
6   Forestay
7   Receiving antenna
8   RBM receiving antenna
9   RDP sense antenna
10   RBK receiving antenna
11   Mk 12/22 radar antennae
12   RDF corrector
13   TAJ transmitting antenna
14   Backstay
15   RAK receiving antenna
16   RAL receiving antenna
17   Whip antenna
18   ECM 'sword'

F2

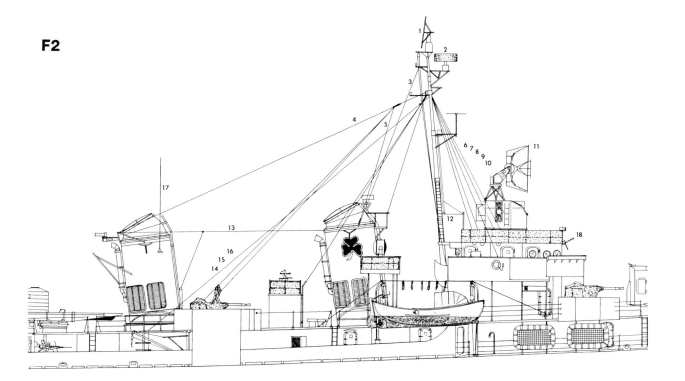

F Rig

F3   RIG (1959)
1   UHF antenna
2   UHF antenna
3   UHF antenna (p & s)
4   AN/SPS-10
5   AS177/UPX antenna
6   Truck light
7   AN/SPS-6C
8   UPX antenna
9   Forestay
10 Receiving antenna
11 LORAN
12 TCS antenna
13 SBT whip antenna
14 Mk 25 radar
15 Whip antenna
16 TBL antenna
17 TED/RED antenna
18 AS/570 antenna (s)
19 AS/571 antenna (p)
20 ECM antenna

F3

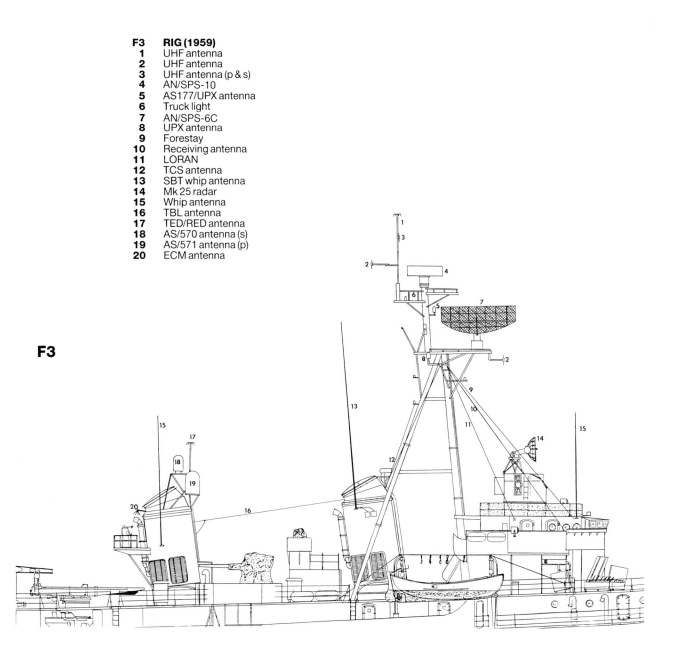

G Armament

G1/1

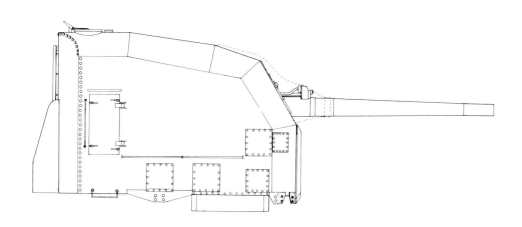

G1/2

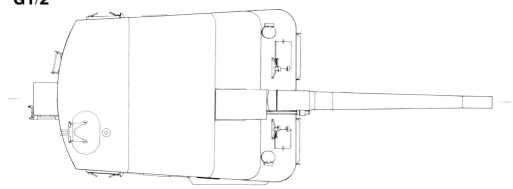

G1/3

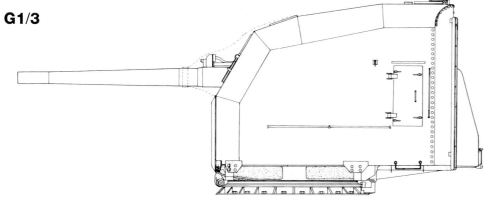

G1/4

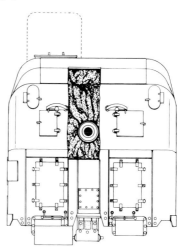

G1	**5in/38 Mk 30 Mod 30 MOUNT** **(1/64 scale)**
G1/1	**Starboard elevation**
G1/2	**Top view**
G1/3	**Port elevation**
G1/4	**Front view**
G1/5	**Rear view**

G1/5

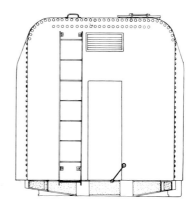

G Armament

G2 5in/38 Mk 30 Mod 18 (1/64 scale)

G2/1 Port elevation

G2/2 Top view

G2/3 Starboard elevation

G2/4 Rear view

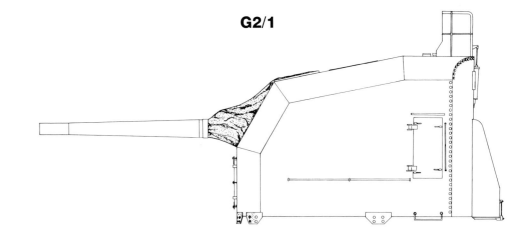

G2/1

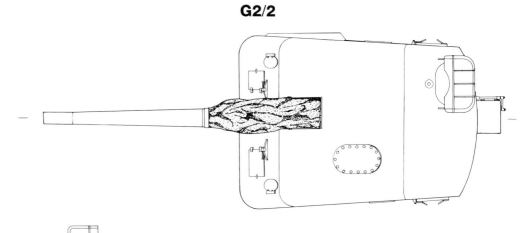

G2/2

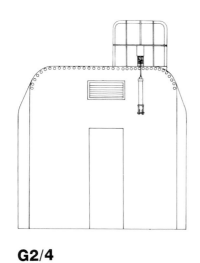

G2/4

G2/3

G3

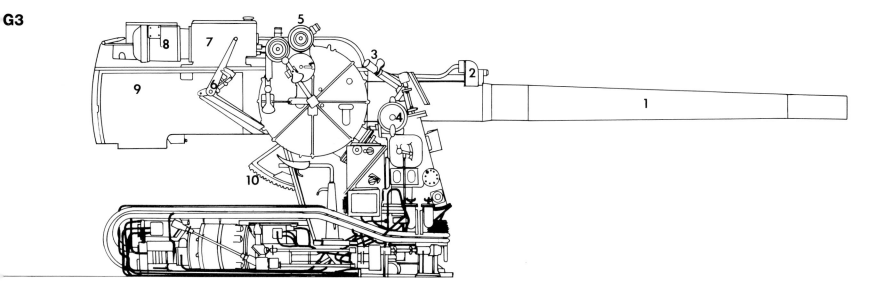

G4

G3   5in/38 Mk 12 Mod 1 (1/32 scale)
1   Barrel
2   Recuperator
3   Telescopic sight
4   Training gear
5   Sight Mk 31 Mod 5
6   Hand operating lever
7   Rammer gear housing
8   Rammer motor
9   Slide
10 Elevating arc

**G4   5in/38 SHELL, ANTI-AIRCRAFT,
COMMON (1/20 scale)**

G Armament

G5 **5in/38 Mk 12 RAMMER CONTROLS**
1 Barrel
2 Operating lever
3 Rammer gear housing
4 Rammer motor
5 Cam plate
6 Spade release lever
7 Spade
8 Case stop
9 Carriage

G6 **STAND AND CARRIAGE FOR 5in/ 38 Mk 12**
1 Gun carriage
2 Trunnion bearing
3 Depression stop
4 Elevation stop
5 Center plate
6 Training pinion gear housing
7 Platform

G5

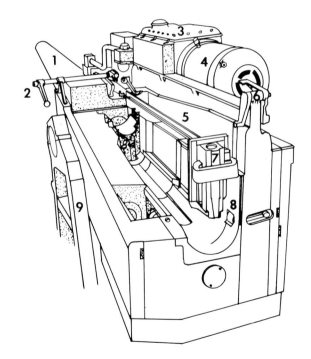

G6

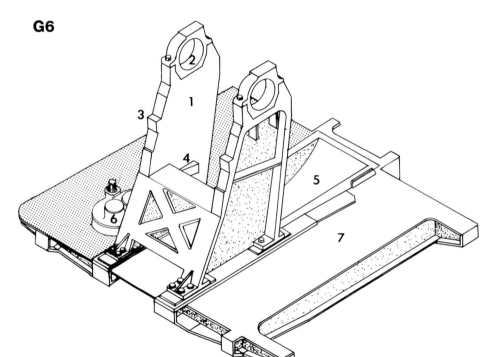

G7   BREECH HAND OPERATING LEVER DETAILS, 5in/38
1   Slide
2   Rammer motor
3   Rammer gear housing
4   Hand operating lever
5   Lever catch
6   Connecting link
7   Elevating arc

G8   BREECHBLOCK AND EXTRACTORS, 5in/38
1   Lip
2   Firing pin
3   Pallet
4   Bearing block ways
5   Outer lug
6   Shelf
7   Seal

G9   5in/38 PRACTICE LOADING MACHINE

G7

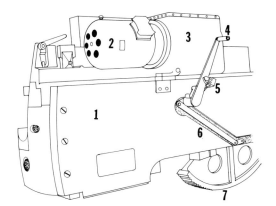

G8

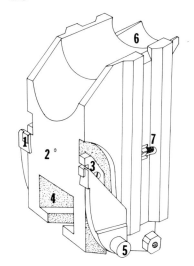

G9

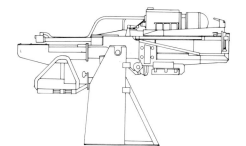

G Armament

G10/1

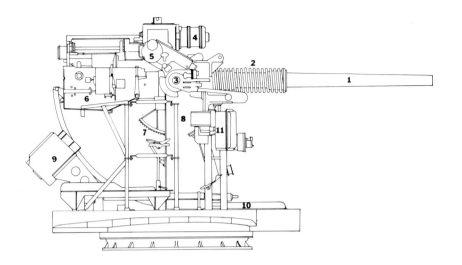

G10/2

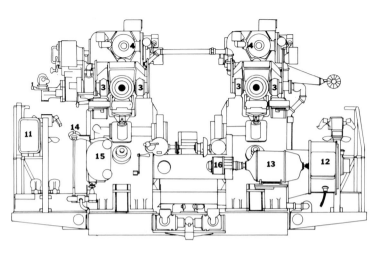

G10/3

G10 **3in/50 Mk 27 TWIN MOUNT (1/64 scale)**

G10/1 Starboard elevation

G10/2 Front view

G10/3 Port elevation
1 Barrel
2 Spring
3 Trunnion bearings
4 Motor
5 Sight setting mechanism
6 Slide
7 Elevating arc
8 Carriage
9 3in/50 ready service magazine
10 Shell ejection chute
11 Training mechanism
12 Elevating mechanism
13 Elevation drive motor
14 Train cable twist indicator
15 Fire interrupter housing
16 Brake release mechanism

G11 **3in/50 ANTI-AIRCRAFT ROUND (1/10 scale)**

G11/1 Complete round

G11/2 Longitudinal section
1 VT fuse
2 Adapter
3 Auxiliary detonating fuse
4 Cast TNT
5 Rotating band
6 Casing
7 Distance piece
8 Wad
9 Smokeless powder
10 Ignition primer

G11/1   G11/2

G12 3in/50 ON-MOUNT READY SERVICE MAGAZINE

G12/1 Mk 1 Mod 1
1   Drum
2   Rotor
3   Rotor shaft
4   Bracket

G12/2 Mk 2 Mod 1

G13 3in/50 LEFT GUNLAYER'S CONTROLS
1   Gunlayer's sight
2   Control unit
3   Fire cutout control

G14 3in/50 MOUNT CAPTAIN'S CONTROLS
1   Left loader indicator panel
2   Right loader indicator panel
3   Selector ASF
4   Selector GSS
5   Selector FSS
6   Gunlaying emergency stop control
7   Left loader master pushbutton
8   Right loader master pushbutton

G13

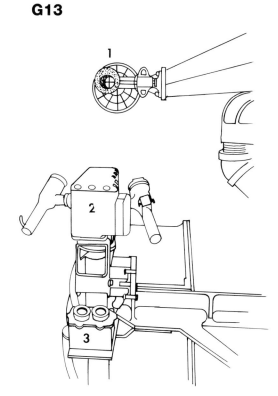

G12/1

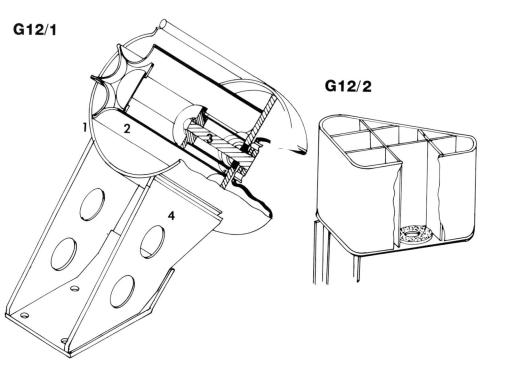

G12/2

G14

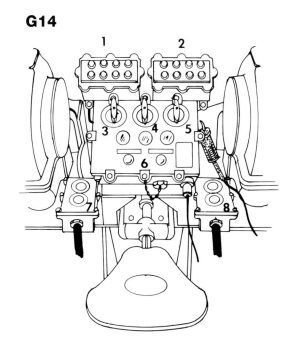

G Armament

G15 3in/50 RIGHT GUNLAYER'S CONTROLS
1. Telescope
2. Open sight
3. Gunlaying control panel
4. Control unit
5. Telescope illumination control rheostat
6. Train cable twist indicator

G16 3in/50 SIGHT SETTER'S STATION
1. Range and sight angle dial
2. Sight angle handwheel
3. Telescope
4. Gun elevation scale
5. Gun elevation pointer
6. Sight illumination control on-off switch

G15

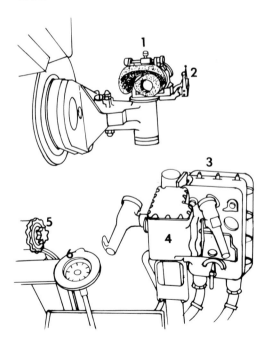

G16

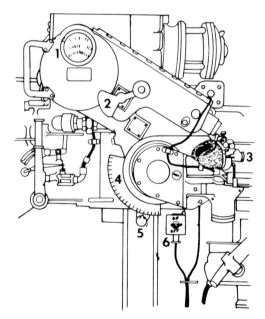

G17   TWIN 40mm Mk 1 MOUNT (1/32 scale)

G17/1 Top view

G17/1 Starboard elevation

1   Open sight for trainer
2   Spring
3   Barrel
4   Flash guard
5   Open sight for elevator
6   Elevator's seat
7   Trainer's seat
8   Sight bar
9   Training handwheel
10 Elevation handwheel
11 Firing pedal
12 Footrests
13 Hydraulic lines
14 Training gear
15 Platform
16 Cooling pump
17 Shell chute
18 Base

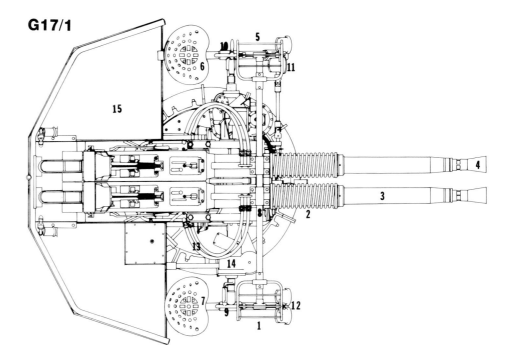

G17/1

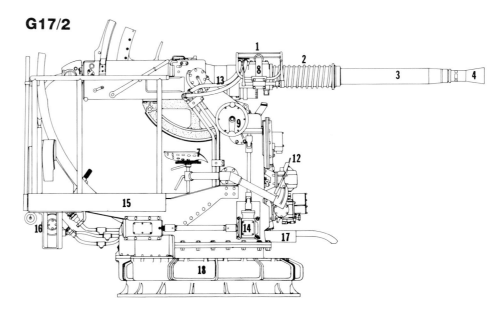

G17/2

G Armament

G18 40mm RING SIGHT (1/10 scale)

G18/1 Front view

G18/2 Side view

G19 40mm SIGHT BAR COMPLETE
        (1/32 scale)

G18/1   **G18/2**

G19

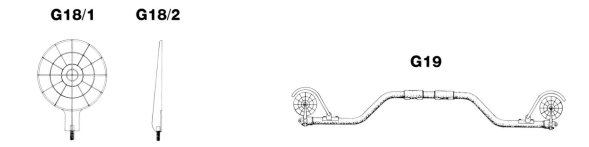

G20 40mm SLIDE AND LOADER
      ARRANGEMENT (no scale)
  1   Recoil cylinder
  2   Recoil piston rod mount
  3   Firing plunger
  4   Trunnion
  5   Top door
  6   Side door
  7   Front guide
  8   Loader guide and pawls
  9   Rear guide
 10   Firing selector lever
 11   Case deflector

G20

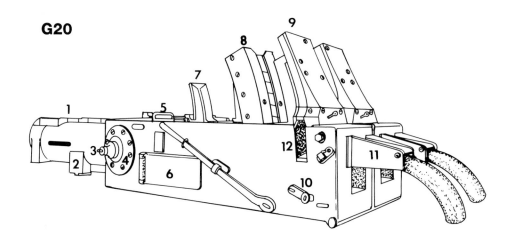

G21 LOADER, 40mm (no scale)
1 Front guide
2 Right loader frame
3 Rear guide
4 Slide
5 Stop pawls
6 Feed pawls
7 Star wheel
8 Star-wheel catch
9 Rammer tray

G22 RAMMER TRAY, 40mm (no scale)
1 Securing bolt hole
2 Rammer tray pawl
3 Guide for feed pawl roller
4 Rammer lever
5 Rammer shoe guide
6 Rammer lever slot

G23 BREECH MECHANISM, 40mm (no scale)
1 Housing
2 Gun barrel catch control arm
3 Breechblock
4 Operating spring case
5 Rammer tray
6 Outer cocking lever
7 Extractor shaft hole
8 Recoil piston rod bolt hole
9 Roller
10 Crankshaft

G24 40mm ROUND, ANTI-AIRCRAFT (1/10 scale)

G24/1 Complete round

G24/2 Longitudinal section
1 Point detonating fuse
2 Cast TNT
3 Rotating band
4 Distance piece
5 Case
6 Percussion primer

G21

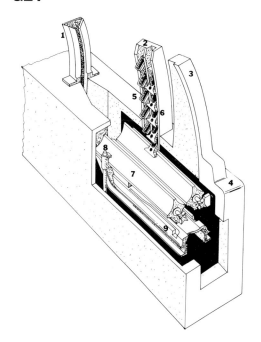

G22

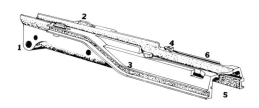

G23

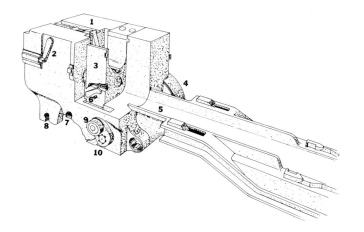

G24/1   G24/2

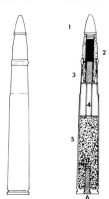

G Armament

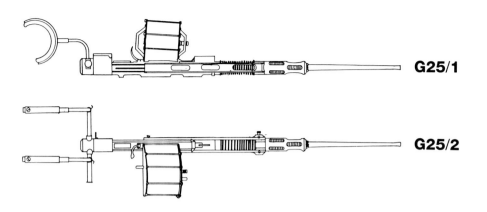

G25/1

G25/2

G25   20mm/70 Mk 4 (1/32 scale)

G25/1 Elevation

G25/2 Top view

G26   20mm MOUNT, Mk 4 (1/32 scale)

G26/1 Elevation, with mount for Mk 14 gunsight

G26/2 Elevation, showing mount at maximum height

G26/3 Top view

G26/1

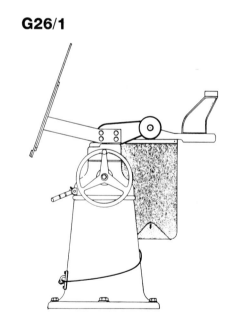

G26/2

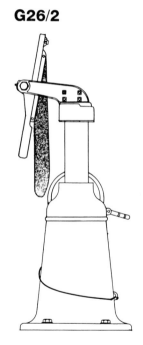

G27   SHIELD FOR 20mm MOUNT Mk 4
(1/32 scale)

G27/1 Front view
1   Shield
2   Rear brace carriage bolts
3   Tie bar

G27/2 Perspective

G27/1

G27/2

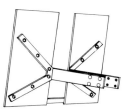

G26/3

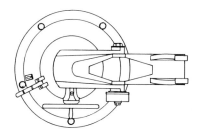

G Armament

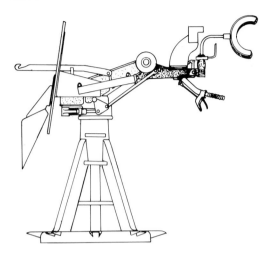

G28/1

G28 **20mm MOUNT, Mk 24 (twin) (1/32 scale)**

G28/1 Elevation

G28/2 Base

G29 **20mm AMMUNITION ($\frac{1}{2}$ scale)**

G29/1 Complete round, anti-aircraft

G29/2 Longitudinal section, anti-aircraft round

G29/3 Longitudinal section, HET

G29/4 Longitudinal section, HEI

G29/5 Longitudinal section, armor-piercing

G28/2

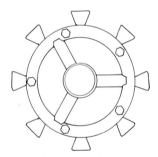

G29/1   **G29/2**   **G29/3**   **G29/4**   **G29/5**

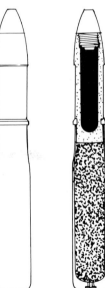
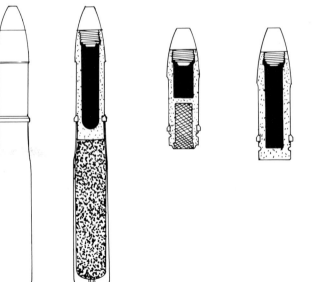

G30   **21in QUINTUPLE TORPEDO TUBE**
      Mk 14 (1/64 scale)

G30/1 Top view

G30/2 Elevation
1. Extension
2. Spoon
3. Barrel
4. Mount
5. Saddle
6. Torpedo course indicator
7. Gyro setter's controls
8. Trainer's bench
9. Depth setting controls
10. Impulse chamber
11. Breech door

G31   **21in QUINTUPLE TORPEDO**
      TUBE, Mk 15 (1/64 scale)

G31/1 Top review

G31/2 Elevation

G30/1

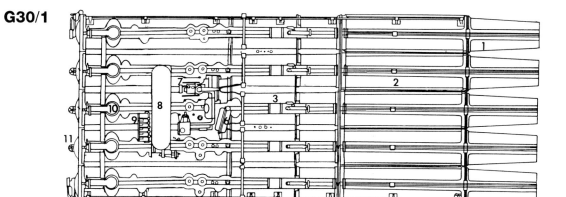

G30/2

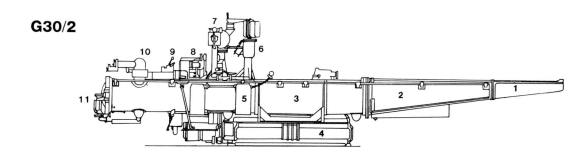

G31/1

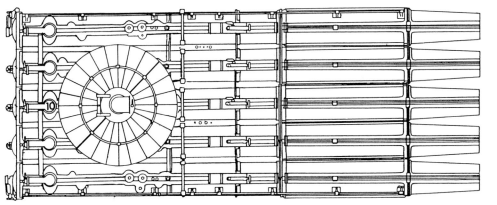

G31/2

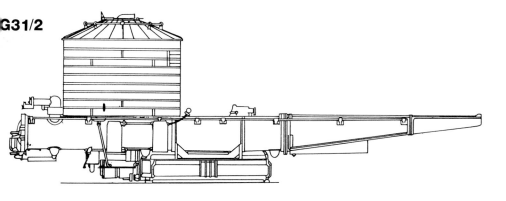

G Armament

G32

G32 21 in TORPEDO, Mk 15 (1/64 scale)
1 Warhead
2 Air flask and fuel
3 Tail section
4 Rudder
5 Contra-rotating propellers

G33

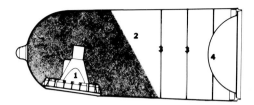

G33 LONGITUDINAL SECTION OF Mk 15 TORPEDO WARHEAD (no scale)
1 Exploder mechanism
2 Cast charge
3 Stiffening rings
4 Bulkhead

G34/1

G34/2

G34/3

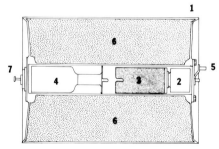

G34 Mk 6 DEPTH CHARGE (1/16 scale

G34/1 Elevation

G34/2 End view

G34/3 Longitudinal section
1 Shell
2 Booster extender
3 Booster
4 Pistol and detonator
5 Safety fork
6 Cast TNT
7 Inlet valve

G35   Mk 9 DEPTH CHARGE (1/16 scale)

G35/1 Elevation

G35/2 Longitudinal section
1   Safety fork
2   Booster extender
3   Booster
4   Detonator
5   Pistol
6   Fins
7   Inlet valve cover

**G36   DEPTH SETTING INDEX DIALS,
        DEPTH CHARGE Mk 9 (1/16 scale)**
1   Index pointer
2   Deep firing pointer
3   Index plate

**G37   DEPTH CHARGE TRACK, Mk 3
        (no scale)**

G35/1

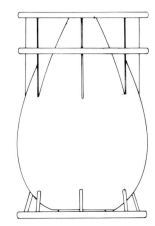

G35/2

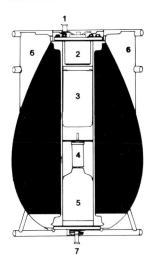

G36

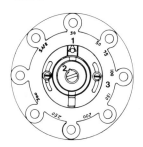

G37

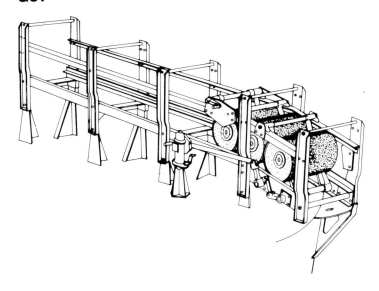

99

G Armament

G38 DEPTH CHARGE PROJECTOR,
Mk 6 (no scale)
1 Base
2 Expansion chamber
3 Tube
4 Breech mechanism
5 Percussion igniter
6 Arbor with tray

G39 ARBOR WITH TRAY (no scale)
1 Sleeve
2 Tray

G40 READY SERVICE RACK FOR Mk 6
PROJECTOR (double; no scale)
1 Arbor storage
2 Loading tray
3 Main frame

G38

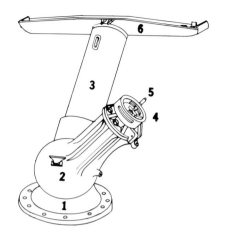

G39

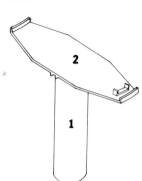

G40

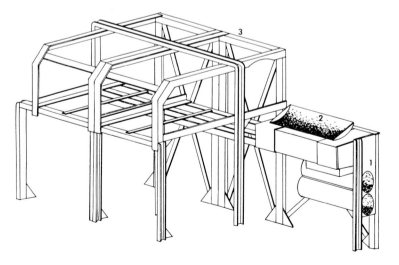

**G41 7.2in PROJECTOR Mk 10
(HEDGEHOG)**

**G41/1 Schematic of projector showing
one beam (no scale)**

**G41/2 Schematic of spigot arrangement
(no scale)**
 1 Trunnion, front
 2 Trunnion bearing, front
 3 Spigot
 4 Spigot base
 5 Trunnion, rear
 6 Trunnion bearing, rear
 7 Cradle locking device

G41/3 Isometric view (no scale)

G42 7.2in PROJECTILE (1/20 scale)

G42/1 Complete round, exterior
 1 Impeller
 2 Warhead
 3 Tail tube
 4 Fins

G42/2 Complete round, interior
 1 Impeller cover
 2 Impeller
 3 Detonator
 4 Charge
 5 Propelling charge
 6 Tail tube
 7 Fins

G41/1

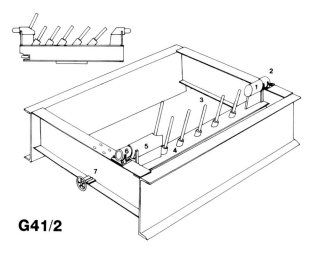

G41/2

G41/3

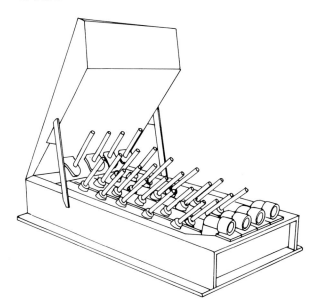

G42/1   G42/2

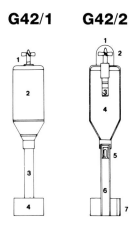

101

H Fire control

H1 **Mk 37 DIRECTOR (1/128 scale)**

H1/1 **Mod 11, top view**

H1/2 **Mod 11, starboard elevation**

H1/3 **Mod 11, front view**

H1/4 **Mod 17, top view**

H1/5 **Mod 17, port elevation**

H1/6 **Mod 17, front view**

1 Shield Mk 2
2 Rangefinder
3 Spotting hatch
4 Telescope hatch
5 Mount captain's cupola
6 Grab rails
7 Blister for Mk 12 radar equipment
8 Blister for Mk 22 radar equipment

H1/1

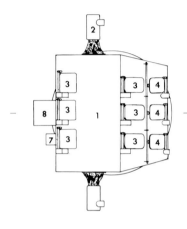

H1/2

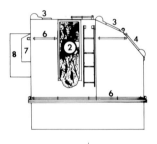

H1/3

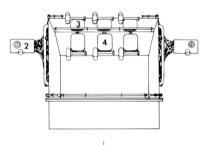

H1/4

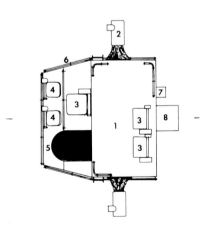

H1/5

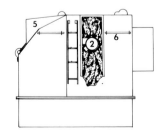

H1/6

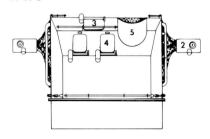

H2   Mk 12 RADAR ANTENNA (1/64 scale)

H2/1   Front view

H2/2   Elevation

H2/1

H2/2

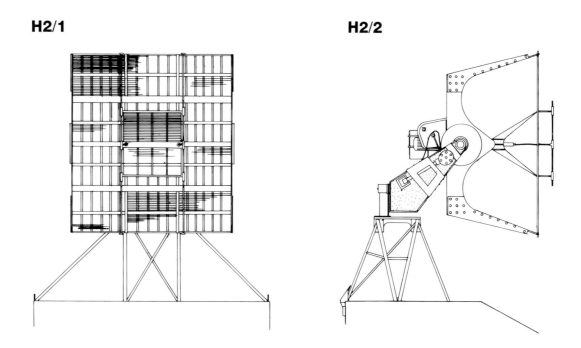

H Fire control

H3 Mk 25 RADAR ANTENNA (1/20 scale)

H3/1 Top view

H3/2 Elevation

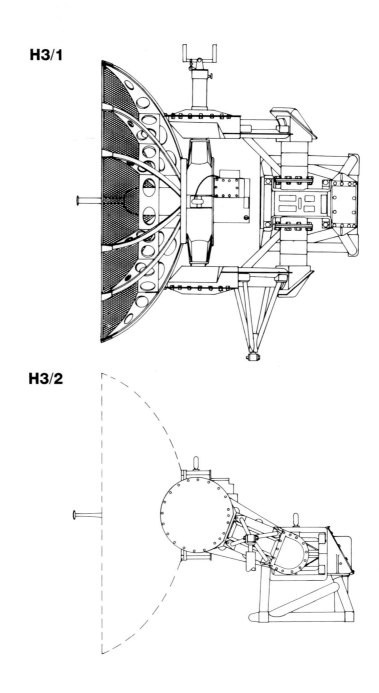

H3/1

H3/2

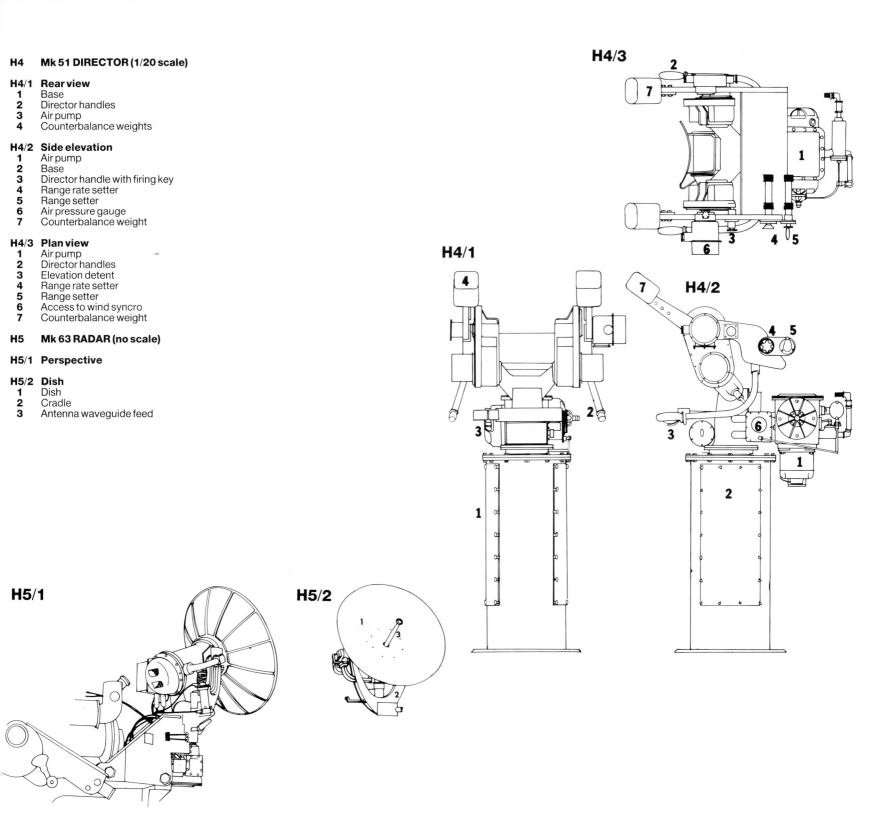

H4   Mk 51 DIRECTOR (1/20 scale)

H4/1 Rear view
1   Base
2   Director handles
3   Air pump
4   Counterbalance weights

H4/2 Side elevation
1   Air pump
2   Base
3   Director handle with firing key
4   Range rate setter
5   Range setter
6   Air pressure gauge
7   Counterbalance weight

H4/3 Plan view
1   Air pump
2   Director handles
3   Elevation detent
4   Range rate setter
5   Range setter
6   Access to wind syncro
7   Counterbalance weight

H5   Mk 63 RADAR (no scale)

H5/1 Perspective

H5/2 Dish
1   Dish
2   Cradle
3   Antenna waveguide feed

H4/3

H4/1

H4/2

H5/1

H5/2

▍ Fittings

I1/1

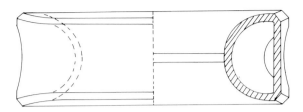

I1/2

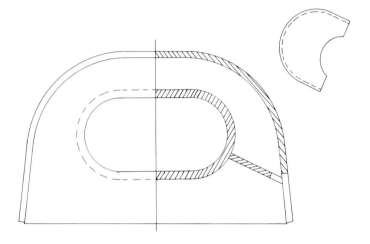

I2/1

I2/2

I2/3

I3/1

I3/3

I3/2

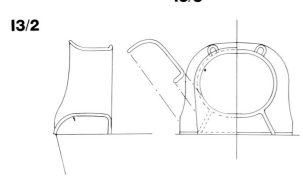

I4/1

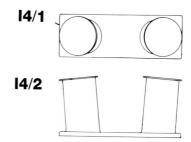

I4/2

I3	**STERN CHOCK (no scale)**
I3/1	**Top view**
I3/2	**Side view**
I3/3	**Front view**
I4	**BOLLARDS (1/32 scale)**
I4/1	**Top view**
I4/2	**Side view**

I5	**WATERTIGHT DOOR (no scale)**	
I5/1	**Typical door**	
	1	Coaming
	2	Dog
	3	Hinge
	4	Handle
I5/2	**Dog arrangement**	
I5/3	**Type B catch for scuttles and hatches**	

I5/1

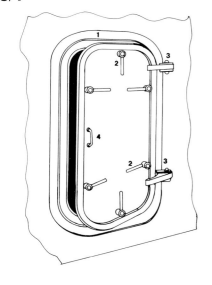

I5/2

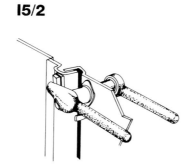

I5/3

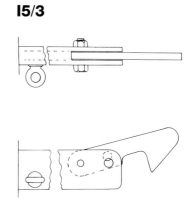

I Fittings

I6/1

I6/2

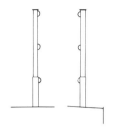

I6/3

I6/4

I7/1

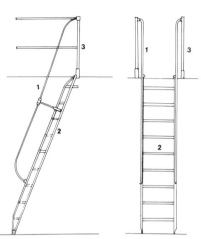

I7/2

I6/5

I8

I9

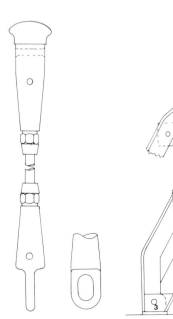
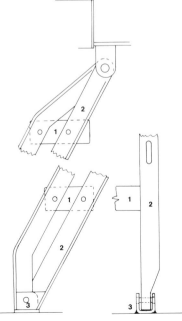

I10

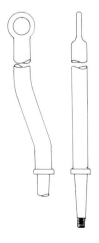

I6	**RAILING STANCHIONS (no scale)**
I6/1	**Type F**
I6/2	**Type D**
I6/3	**Type C**
I6/4	**Type G**
I6/5	**Type H–1**
I7	**INCLINED LADDER (typical)**
I7/1	**Side view**
I7/2	**Front view**
1	Railing
2	Ladder
3	Stanchion
I8	**WIRE ROPE HAND RAIL FITTINGS (no scale)**
I9	**TYPICAL LADDER DETAILS (no scale)**
1	Tread
2	Side frame
3	Clip
I10	**TYPICAL BENT STANCHION (no scale)**

I12

I11

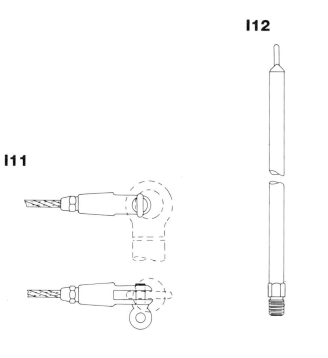

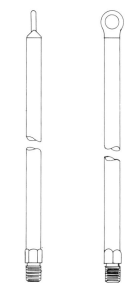

I11 **GUARD RAIL CLEVIS (no scale)**

I12 **TYPICAL STRAIGHT STANCHION (no scale)**

I13 **CLIP FOR WIRE ROPE CLEVIS (no scale)**

I14 **TYPICAL WIRE ROPE AND STANCHION AROUND DECK HATCH (no scale)**

I15 **SIDE LADDER (fitted post-World War II; no scale)**

I15/1 **Side view**

I15/2 **Top view**
1 Platform
2 Ladder
3 Landing platform
4 Ladder support stanchion

I15/2

I13

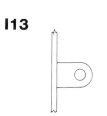

I15/1

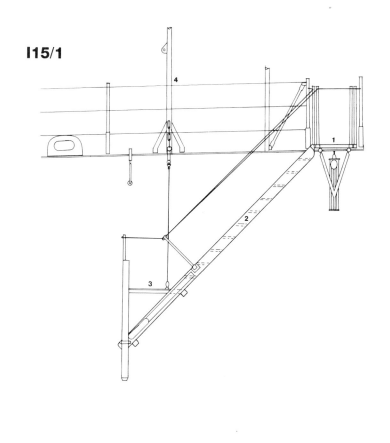

I14

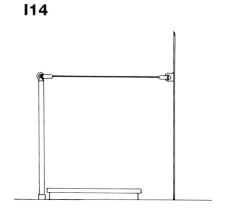

I Fittings

I16

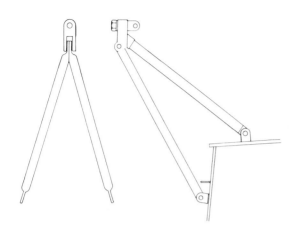

I17/1

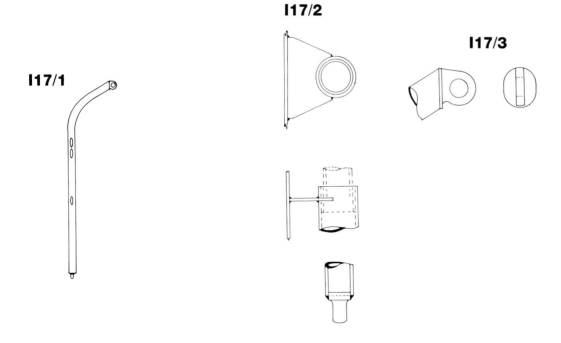

I17/2

I17/3

I16   **LADDER SUPPORT FRAME (no scale)**

I17   **DEPTH CHARGE DAVIT (no scale)**

I17/1 **Davit**

I17/2 **Davit bracket**

I17/3 **Davit head**

I18   **FIRE PLUG (no scale)**
  1 Bracket
  2 Nozzle
  3 Hose
  4 Wyegate
  5 Self-cleaning strainer
  6 Adjustable spanner
  7 Fire plug

I19   **SELF-CLEANING STRAINER FOR FIRE NOZZLE (no scale)**
  1 $2\frac{1}{2}$in inlet
  2 $2\frac{1}{2}$in outlet
  3 Operating handle
  4 Strainer
  5 Flushing outlet

I20   **TYPE A REEL (no scale)**

I20/1 **Side view**
  1 End plate
  2 Lightening hole
  3 Support bracket
  4 Brake

I20/2 **Front view**
  1 End plate
  2 Support bracket
  3 Reel drum
  4 Axle
  5 Wire rope

I21   **TYPE B REEL (no scale)**

I21/1 **Side view**
  1 End plate
  2 Lightening hole
  3 Support bracket
  4 Brake

I21/2 **Front view**
  1 End plate
  2 Support bracket
  3 Drum
  4 Axle
  5 Separators

I18

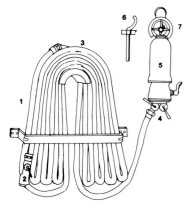

I19

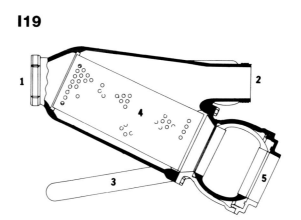

I20/1

I20/2

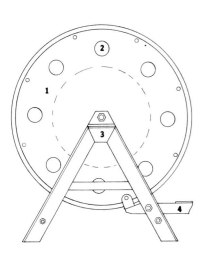

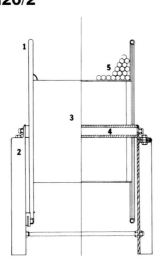

I21/1

I21/2

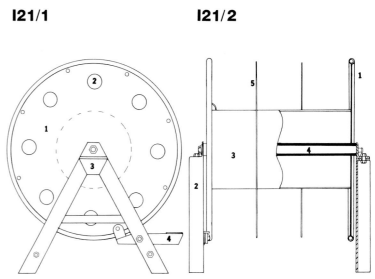

I Fittings

I22 **FANFARE REEL (fitted post-World War II; no scale)**

I23 **FLOATER NET BASKET WITH A SECTION OF NET** (no scale)

I24 **RAISED WATERTIGHT ESCAPE SCUTTLE WITH DAVIT SOCKET** (no scale)

I22

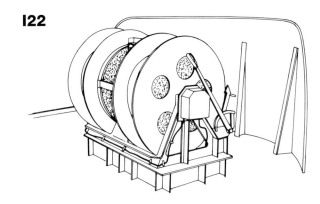

I23

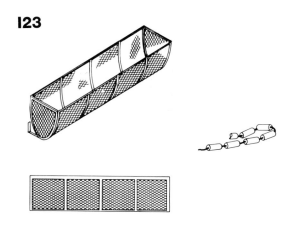

I24

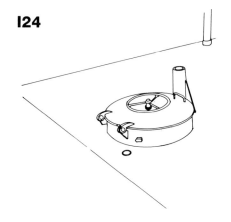

I25   REAR VIEW OF STACK (no scale)

I26   AFT BOAT DAVIT (1/64 scale)

I26

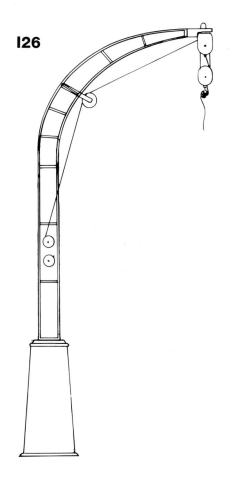

I25

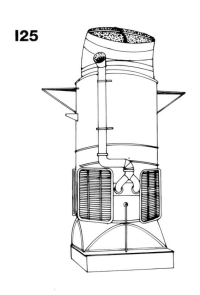

113

J Ground tackle

J1 **CHAIN PIPE END COVER AND DOG ASSEMBLY (drawings in this section are typical and not reproduced to a specific scale)**

J2 **CHAIN PIPE END COVER STRONGBACK**

J1

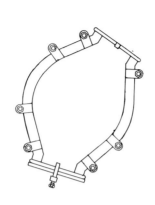

J2

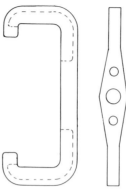

J3 **BELLMOUTH FOR CHAINPIPE**

J3/1 **Plan view**

J3/2 **Side view**

J3/3 **Section**

J4 **COMPRESSOR BOX**

J4/1 **Sectional view**

J4/2 **Side elevation**

J5 **COMPRESSOR**

J3/1

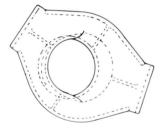

J3/3

J4/1   **J4/2**

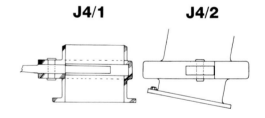

J5

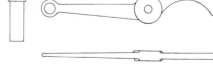

J3/2

J6/2

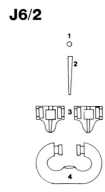

J7

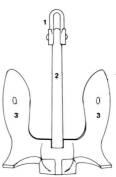

J6   **DETACHABLE LINK**

J6/1 **Assembled**
1   Lead ball
2   Tapered forelock pin
3   Lugged forelock
4   Link body

J6/2 **Disassembled**
1   Lead ball
2   Forelock pin
3   Forelock
4   Link body

J7   **STOCKLESS ANCHOR**

J8   **PAD EYE**

J9   **TOWING BRIDLE**

J9/1 **Plan view**

J9/2 **Side view**
1   Pad eye
2   Detachable link
3   Turnbuckle
4   Pelican hook
5   Shackle
6   Wire bridle

J6/1

J8

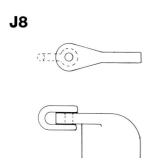

J9/1

J9/2

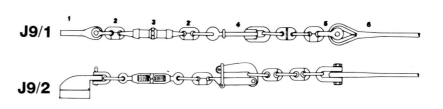

K Ship's boats

K1 **26ft MOTOR WHALEBOAT** *The Sullivans* carried two standard motor whaleboats Mk 1. There were a number of versions of this Mark which were used interchangeably, two of which are presented in this section (1/40 scale)

K1/1 Plan view, decked version

K1/2 Outboard profile, decked version, showing outline of canopy

K1/3 Outboard profile, undecked version

K1/4 Plan view, undecked version
1. Bench seat
2. Storage
3. Motor cover for DA motor
4. Mechanic's position
5. Muffler
6. Tiller
7. Rudder

K1/5 Inboard profile, undecked version
1. Sampson post
2. Lifting eye
3. Motor cover
4. DA moor
5. Muffler
6. Propeller shaft
7. Helmsman's position

K1/1

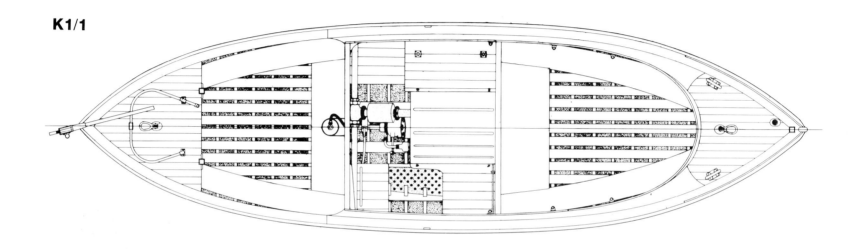

K1/2

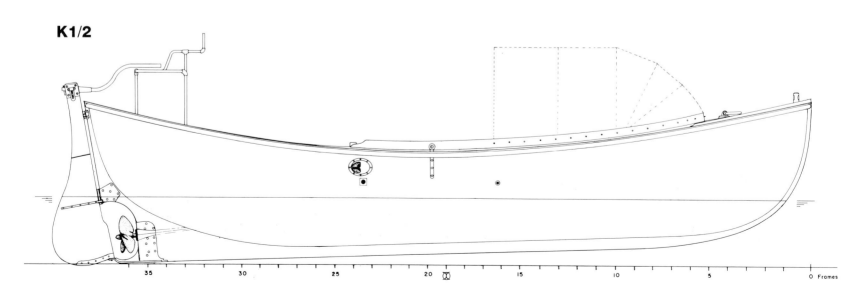

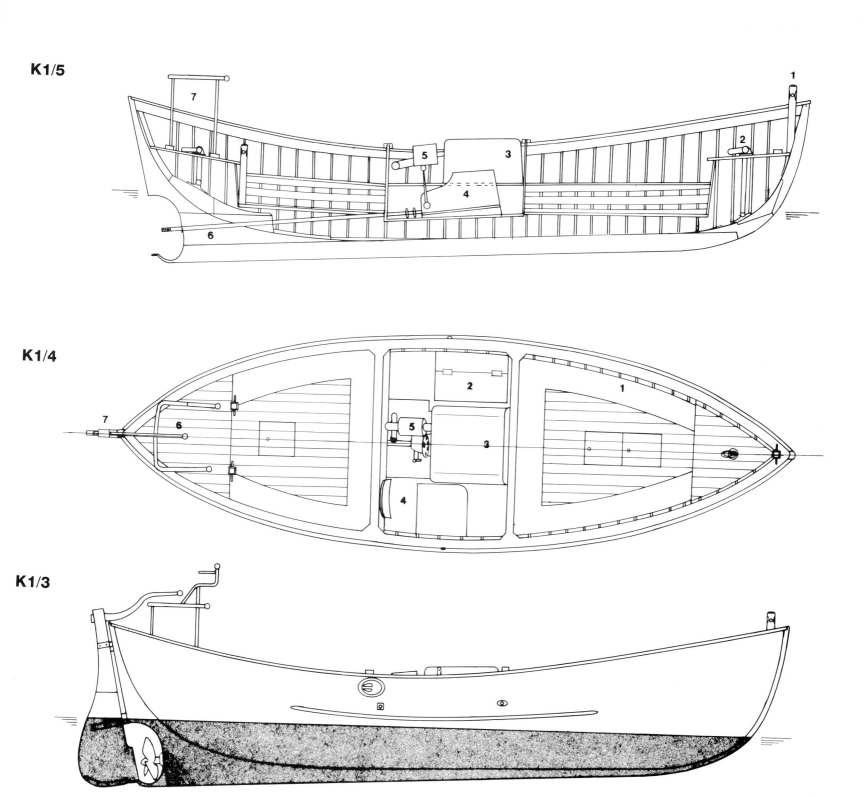

K1/5

K1/4

K1/3

K Ship's boats

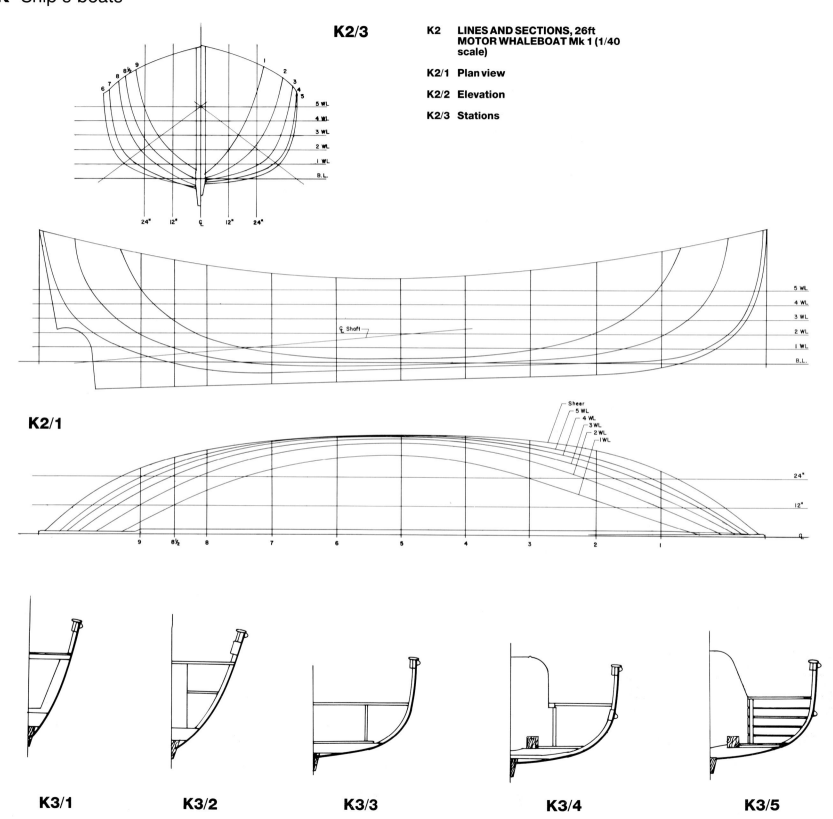

K2/3

K2   LINES AND SECTIONS, 26ft MOTOR WHALEBOAT Mk 1 (1/40 scale)

K2/1   Plan view

K2/2   Elevation

K2/3   Stations

5 WL
4 WL
3 WL
2 WL
1 WL
B.L.

24"   12"   ℄   12"   24"

5 WL
4 WL
3 WL
2 WL
1 WL
B.L.

℄ Shaft

K2/1

Sheer
5 WL
4 WL
3 WL
2 WL
1 WL

24"

12"

9   8½   8   7   6   5   4   3   2   1

K3/1   **K3/2**   **K3/3**   **K3/4**   **K3/5**

K3 **LONGITUDINAL SECTIONS, 26ft MOTOR WHALEBOAT Mk 1, undecked (1/40 scale)**

K3/1 Frame 3 looking forward

K3/2 Frame 5 looking forward

K3/3 Frame 15 looking forward

K3/4 Frame 17 looking aft

K3/5 Frame 19 looking forward

K3/6 Frame 23 looking aft

K3/7 Frame 25 looking forward

K3/8 Frame 28 looking forward

K3/9 Frame 32 looking aft

K3/10 Frame 33 looking aft

K4 **LIFTING ARRANGEMENT (no scale)**
1 Double block
2 Raymond releasing hook
3 Lifting eye
4 Lifting eye support

K5 **RAYMOND RELEASING HOOK (no scale)**
1 Block body
2 Sheave
3 Sheave pin
4 Main hook
5 Lifting eye
6 Safety hook

K4

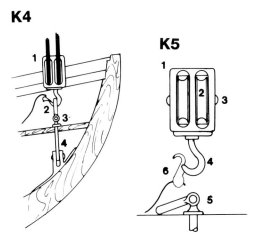

K5

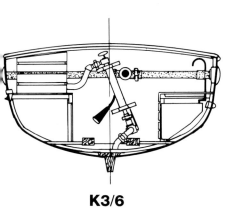

K3/6

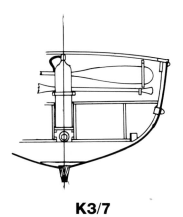

K3/7

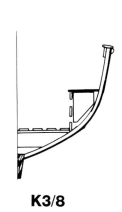

K3/8

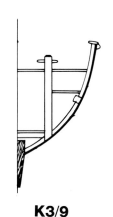

K3/9

K3/10